Susan G Horn

The Next World

Fifty-Six Communications from Eminent Historians, Authors, Legislators, etc., Now

in Spirit-Life

Susan G Horn

The Next World

Fifty-Six Communications from Eminent Historians, Authors, Legislators, etc., Now in Spirit-Life

ISBN/EAN: 9783744719223

Printed in Europe, USA, Canada, Australia, Japan

Cover: Foto ©Thomas Meinert / pixelio.de

More available books at **www.hansebooks.com**

THE NEXT WORLD.

Fifty-six Communications

FROM

EMINENT HISTORIANS, AUTHORS, LEGISLATORS, ETC.,
NOW IN SPIRIT-LIFE.

THROUGH

MRS. SUSAN G. HORN.

"*And often, from that other world on this
Some gleams from great souls gone before may shine.*"
—J. RUSSELL LOWELL.

London:
JAMES BURNS, 15, SOUTHAMPTON ROW, W.C.

1890.

CONTENTS.

	PAGE
Introduction	vii

THE NEXT WORLD		1
PRINCE ALBERT . . .	*England and the Queen*	3
HARRIETT MARTINEAU .	*Life in the Spirit-World* . . .	9
CHARLES KINGSLEY . .	*Reform in Spirit-Life*	16
JUDGE EDMONDS . . .	*The Two States: Real and Ideal* .	20
JUDGE EDMONDS . . .	*Rich Men of New York*	25
JOHN STUART MILL . .	*Immortality*	31
HORACE GREELEY . . .	*Home of Horace Greeley*	34
PROFESSOR AGASSIZ . .	*Evolution*	44
SECRETARY SEWARD . . . *Statesmanship from a Spiritual Standpoint*		49
BULWER (LORD LYTTON)	*Metempsychosis*	55
TITIAN	*Art Notes*	59
ABRAHAM LINCOLN . .	*My Passage to Spirit-Life* . . .	62
CHARLOTTE CUSHMAN .	*Death by Fire*	67
EDWIN FORREST . . .	*Present State of the Drama* . .	72
CHARLES DICKENS . .	*Christmas Carols*	75
DE QUINCEY	*An Opium-eater's Dream of Heaven*	80
FANNY FERN	*Spirit-Flowers*	84
HANS CHRISTIAN ANDERSEN	*The Story of the Great King* . .	87
GEORGES SAND	*Chateau in the midst of Roses* . .	93
MRS. GASKELL	*The Spirit-Bride*	97
FENNIMORE COOPER . .	*Lone Star: an Indian Spirit's Story*	101
HERODOTUS	*Pre-historic Man*	113
GEO. SMITH (Assyriologist)	*Explorations: Assyrian & Spiritual*	117

Contents.

		PAGE
Dr. Livingstone . . .	Leaves from my Spirit Journal .	120
Victor Emanuel . . .	Italy and the Church	123
The Pope	Bless, and curse not!	125
Theirs	To the Republic of France . . .	127
G. H. Lewes	Epic of the Soul	129
William Howitt . . .	Christianity and Spiritualism . .	137
George Thompson . .	A Call to Freedom	142
Princess Alice . . .	An Appeal on behalf of Children .	145
Ralph Waldo Emerson	Philosophy: Ancient and Modern .	147
Lord Beaconsfield . .	The Political Situation in England	150
George Eliot	A Change from Materialism . .	154
Dean Stanley . . .	Spiritualism: the True and False.	158
Garibaldi	The Liberator of Italy	162
Charles Darwin . . .	The Law of Creation	164
Mary, Queen of Scots .	Destiny	168
Gambetta	For France and Freedom! . . .	171
Wagner	The Music of the Future . . .	176
Longfellow	Outre Mer! Outre Terre! . . .	181
Jane Carlyle	A Tribute to Thomas Carlyle . .	185
Benjamin Franklin .	Spiritual Aphorisms	191
Egypt	Pre-Historic Ages	197
Thomas Carlyle . . .	The Folly of Hero-Worship . . .	200
James T. Brady . . .	The Cause and Treatment of Crime	205
Peter Cooper . . . . Educational Institutions in the Spirit-World		212
Robert Bruce	Spiritualism, A Liberator . . .	216
Czar of Russia . . .	The Autocrat's Doom	219
Lord Frederick Cavendish Capital Punishment Condemned		221
Karl Friedrich Zöllner	Spiritual State of Germany . . .	223
Cromwell Fleetwood Varley Astronomical Origin of Spiritual Phenomena		226
J. W. Colenso	Mistaken Policy of the Church . .	232
Judge Edmonds . . .	The Spirit-Editor's Valedictory. .	235
A Stranger	Visit to the Spirit-World . . .	241

PUBLISHER'S PREFACE.

A previous volume, given through the mediumship of Mrs. Horn, entitled *Strange Visitors*, was so interesting, that it gave pleasure to learn that another volume of a similar kind was in preparation, and that the spirit editor, "Judge Edmonds," desired that it should be placed in our hands for publication. The matter was found to be insufficient to form a volume of the kind intended, and during the movements of the medium, to secure favourable conditions for receiving further communications, much time was exhausted, as the dates appended indicate. The localities subjoined to the several articles testify to the great extent of travel involved in preparing the book.

Ultimately, during a visit to London, Mrs. Horn became our guest, a condition which seemed essential to the production of several of the articles. Having seen the book through the press, and some of it having been produced under our observation, we can testify to its being a genuine mediumistic production, given as truly stated in the introductory notes. Generally the medium was controlled to write, but sometimes the matter was dictated while Mrs. Horn was under influence, her impersonations being strictly in accordance with the character communicating. In some instances the presence of the communicating spirits was noted by others before the control of Mrs. Horn was effected, thus furnishing corroborative testimony of spirit action. The papers could not be dictated or written at the will of the medium, but at the most unlikely times, as the spirits found conditions suitable for their purpose.

Publisher's Preface.

Several of the papers speak of the modifying conditions influencing matter thus produced, and the part played in the work by the mental bias or capacities of the medium. Yet after due allowance for this, the papers evince great variety of opinion and breadth of mental characteristic, the writers not being fully agreed on such questions as re-incarnation, Christianity, &c. The conluding paper, given anonymously, may be regarded as a sketch illustrative of the operation of spiritual states on human life, rather than in support of assumed historical views.

Though the plates were made several years ago, circumstances have prevented the appearance of the book on this side of the Atlantic, which delay seems to be a part of the plan, as it has enabled many of the forecasts indicated by certain of the writers to become accomplished facts, thereby increasing the importance of the statements recorded.

J. B.

THE NEXT WORLD.

WE know something of this world, of its manners and customs; but of the next—how little, how meagre our information! and yet our friends leave our side year after year and go to the Unseen Land. How do they reach it? we question. Do they walk, ride, or fly? Have they individualised bodies, or are they mere souls, without form or substance? Do they live there as birds in the air, or do they dwell in houses as do we the civilised of earth? Do flowers bloom and trees grow there? and if trees thrive, as the old prophets seemed to have discovered, can they be cut down and formed into articles of use, as here? Can the inhabitants of that unseen world make tables, chairs, and pianos, as well as *harps of gold?* or are they so familiar with the secrets of nature that they can create these desirable forms from the elements by an effort of will? Do they retain their organs of sight, hearing, and of speaking? If they speak, have they tongues and palates? and if so, can they taste, eat, or drink? As is related in the Old Testament, "The Lord smelled a sweet savour" of Noah's sacrifice. Angels (spirits) ate with Abraham when he was promised a son in his old age, and Sarah listening from behind the folds of the tent laughed incredulously.

If they have form and proportion, are they in the habit of clothing themselves as we do? The ancient clairvoyants describe them as "clothed in white raiment;" and we, in our states of trance and in dreams, behold them in customary garments. Whence do they obtain these robes? How is the tissue manufactured? Can it be removed at pleasure, or is it an addendum to the spirit like the wings of a butterfly?

What is the trance state, and how is it superinduced by the inhabitants of the Next World? The medium thus describes this condition: I even approach the trance state with reluctance, and a feeling of awe comes over me as I enter this mysterious condition. The room I am in vanishes; the friends who surround me seem removed an immeasurable distance—no longer part nor parcel with me; I appear to be falling through space; all is darkness about me, when suddenly the air becomes illuminated, like floating points of light, each twinkling with a golden splendour. What transpires around me I only know as a person asleep in a stage coach or a rail-car is conscious that he is travelling—he lifts his heavy eyelids and closes them over a knowledge that a forest of trees skirt the roadside—that hill and plain and smiling river bound the distance, and yet he sleeps.

How are the sensations thus described produced on the clairvoyante?

All these questions pour in upon the mind of the medium, and it is in the endeavour to answer them that the spirits give the following accounts :—

ENGLAND AND THE QUEEN.

PRINCE ALBERT.

THIS genial spirit was among the first to appear. We had heard of Queen Victoria's belief in spirit-intercourse, and had been told that at her own private table she had covers laid for the Prince (her husband) as when he lived on earth, and that when she dined or breakfasted alone his chair was placed opposite hers, and that thus their sweet domestic life was continued between the two worlds. We desired to know how far he realised this loving attention of his wife, and also to learn what position monarchs held in the next world. In answer to our thoughts Prince Albert controlled the medium, and gave the following account of his condition and manner of passing his time. His influence was dignified and yet enlivening; he conversed naturally, and answered questions with apparent pleasure.

December, 1876.

OU, who have visited that ancient pile Windsor Castle, who have walked through its apartments of state, seen the banqueting halls and ghostly chapels of our ancestors, cannot realise that, unseen, I walked by your side and accompanied you in your tour through the rooms,* thinking of the many happy days I had spent with Victoria and our children in this and other palaces of dear old England.

* Referring to a visit made by the Editor to Windsor Castle.

I love England and am interested in her welfare, not as a ruler, but as an adviser and friend. I watch over the councils of the Queen, and I make one of the Cabinet. I attend Parliament, accompanied sometimes by Lords Brougham and Palmerston, and others who have made affairs of State their study in life. I have met there from time to time Pitt and Fox, the Duke of Wellington, and many more who still feel an interest in the welfare of their native land.

Personally I attend the Queen daily; so strong are her mediumistic powers, so perfect is the unison between us two, that I feel as though we had never been separated. I live as it were in two worlds!

Victoria has told the public of our happy home in the Highlands. She delights in natural, simple life, and thinks, as I do, that the ideal monarch should be one with the people, not above them.

The Queen loves Balmoral, and it is because my spirit can visit untrammeled that free mountain-place, that she is drawn thither. If the public could understand the true reason for her choice they would cease to cavil at it.

A portion of time spent among mountains helps to develop a love of freedom, and a true knowledge of the natural equality between men. Spirits also can approach mortals more intimately upon elevated ground, and it is for these reasons that the Queen loves Balmoral, and this is why the true Briton loves to explore mountain-heights.

Some of Victoria's subjects reproach her for not supporting the dignity of the nation by external show; but court pageants are merely pastimes for the ignorant, and tend to blind and subjugate the oppressed by the dazzle and splendour of pomp. A self-poised, cultivated nation should rise above mere childish glitter, and England is gradually doing this.

I think the Queen is right in withdrawing from spectacles which subserve the purpose of diverting the mind from its true necessities and a rightful understanding of its condition. Time was when barbaric shows were necessary accompaniments to the triumphal chariot of the conqueror. Not that I desire to deprecate pleasure where it tends to invigorate and restore too greatly taxed energies; but a useless expenditure of wealth in pageants in the end only cripples the people, and weakens them both in body and mind.

Before our day many kings and queens reigned in England, and I have had the rare happiness of meeting several of them in spirit-life. But are they kings and queens still? No; many have learned that they were unfitted for the positions they held on earth.

But few among them possessed minds of great comprehension, a few only were able to look beyond themselves and perceive the needs of the people over whom they reigned.

Our unfortunate cousin, Charles I., lost his life because he thought only of his immediate wants, and would not listen to the requests of his people. I have met him in spirit-life an altered man.

Progress, and the development of the human race, is the law of the Universe. The Spirit-world controls the earth, it puts forth its unseen hand, and drags from the throne the potentate who would crush the people, and take from them their hard-earned pittance, or push them back into the dark caverns of ignorance.

This is the occult force that overturns nations and empires! It was this mighty spirit-power that drove Marie Antoinette to the block, and tore the triumphant eagle from the banner of Napoleon!

Unhappy Marie Antoinette! her sufferings on earth in some measure atoned for her pride of power! I have seen her in spirit-life, beautified by sorrow, educated by sad experience; living a quiet uneventful life in a tranquil home; no longer queen! no longer hated nor despised!

I have seen Mary Queen of Scots, another unfortunate queen, but possessed of a finer nature than Marie Antoinette, a loving though an erring woman. She leads a more active life of charity than the other Marie. Possessed of a strong love nature, and a subtle magnetic power, she makes herself felt both in the Spirit-world and on earth. She had no desire to oppress the people, she was merely misled by her cravings for a stronger nature than her own to sustain her, and by her desire to be loved and admired.

The two Napoleons are together in spirit-life. They are men of the people. Though temporarily blinded by power, they aimed at the uplifting of the masses. When they tightened their grip on the people, it was loosened by spirit-power, and now they are true democrats. They have many adherents in the world they inhabit, and are still leaders. Possessed of a tremendous energy, they can accomplish great good; their views are large and not self-centred; and though they keep their eye on France, they visit other nations, and study different modes of government.

This wonderful panorama of life interests me deeply. History here walks before me, not in book form, but clothed and living.

I wish to apprise persons holding responsible positions on earth, of the important fact that those who have ruled kingdoms in life cannot return to earth and communicate their thoughts more readily than those who have held the most humble position.

Death is said to be a leveler of distinctions, and such it

would be if the education and information we acquire on earth did not accompany us to the second stage of existence.

Be a man a king or a commoner, if he educates his mind and develops his moral faculties, he will reap the benefit of his earth efforts in the after state. Such has been my happy experience. I rejoice that I gave my attention to belles-lettres, the study of the fine arts, and political economy, and that I used my efforts to advocate the welfare of the people over whom Victoria reigned.

In thus educating my mind and elevating my soul, I prepared myself for an equable enjoyment in the spirit-world. My acquirements have aided me here; the sentiments of faith and trust in a Supreme Power, and the love of humanity which my Consort's true womanly nature fostered, have aided me in securing employment for my faculties in this Land of Immortality! Though this is a world of light and beauty, old associations live actively within my breast, and family ties survive the dissolution of the material body, therefore I pass much of my time in dear old England.

I have before said, if a ruler ceases to look after the interests of the masses—if he forgets that he is placed in power as a guide and father to his subjects—if he forgets these things, he will sooner or later be hurled from his throne, and uprooted from the ground which seems to him so firm.

The step of Justice seems slow in reaching some nations, while it overtakes others with rapidity, but though it be retarded for a time, it cannot be evaded. Already has it reached the Papal dominions; its tread is now shaking the throne of the Ottoman empire!* Wherever there is oppression—wherever there is an attempt to stay the hand of

---

* This article was given some five months previous to the Russo-Turkish War.

Progress and enforce ignorance—there will Justice appear in the form of revolution and war; it is foreordained.

In America your rulers hold a short-lived power; but as true as there is any attempt to oppress the poor, to withhold the influence of public schools and universal education, to draw from any portion of the inhabitants their just prerogatives, or to oppress in any way the masses, you will feel the influence of that spirit-power, which regulates governments and the kingdoms of earth, rebuking and leading you through darkness to a higher form of government!

SKETCH OF
LIFE IN THE SPIRIT-WORLD.

HARRIET MARTINEAU.

THE news had reached America of Harriet Martineau's departure from earth; the question asked was,—Would she come and describe her entrance into the Next World through the medium—would she, who believed there was no hereafter, tell the world how she solved the problem of future existence?

She came like a soft moonbeam; her influence was that of a tranquil, satisfied nature, in harmony with her spirit-life, glad to impart information, and rejoiced to live and speak again in the Next World, and happy to undo, as far as in her power, the baneful influence of her theory of eternal death; though, as she says, the views she expressed stimulated people to investigate and throw aside the rotten creeds of past ages.

N the latter portion of my life on earth I accepted the theory of the non-existence of the soul, as expounded by those eminent investigators into natural causes, viz., Darwin, Huxley, Arnold, Comte, and Herbert Spencer.

I sympathised more eagerly with their views inasmuch as I found that the creeds of theologians concerning the soul and its Creator became but absurd fables when brought beneath the light of science. Many of the years that I lived in the body were passed in physical suffering, but I devoted them to study, seeking vainly to solve the enigma of existence; alas! if I possessed an immortal soul I failed to perceive it, with all my investigations.

In the early days of mesmerism I became a subject of that marvellous agent, and I learned then of the action of one mind over another and the power of will over matter, and I might probably have become a believer in the spiritual philosophy which grew out of it, if it had been possible to demonstrate to my senses the existence of spirit. The discoveries in clairvoyance I looked upon as the subtle action of unrecognised forces of Nature, and the more I investigated the more apparent it became to me that the so-called spirit and matter were identical, and therefore not immortal.

But now I find that the science of magnetic control, as discovered by Mesmer, and occult influences are as old as man, and are the connecting link between the world of spirits and the world of matter. I now discover that the action of the mysterious passes which produce such peculiar effects upon the human frame, is controlled by laws as wise and simple as those that govern the office of breathing.

The science of mesmerism is not fully understood in the present day, nor is it practised as effectually as it was centuries prior to the Christian era; if it were, communication with the Spirit-world would be of more frequent occurrence; it is now one of the lost arts, but it is being gradually restored.

Few persons understand the reason why disease is cured by magnetic passes; I will try and explain the cause. There is a force latent in man termed by the great investigator Reichenbach OD FORCE, which appears like an electric light issuing from the body. The brain is the focus of this force and is capable, by its will-power, of extending or contracting it. Disease causes a declension of the will-power, and the non-emission of the light in certain portions of the body follows; the mesmeric physician infuses his aura and will-power into the negative portion of the patient's body, the od force becomes equally distributed, and health is the result.

But respecting these matters I only groped in the dark while on earth. Now all is changed, and "how great is the change!" Since I entered the Spirit-world my faculties of hearing and taste have been restored, and like a new being I have commenced upon a new sphere of existence.

How beautiful this Spirit-world is no tongue can tell! I would fain describe the sensations I felt upon closing my eyes on earth, expecting to sink back into utter darkness and annihilation, when I found myself *conscious* in an atmosphere of light, and in the midst of a landscape of the most wonderful beauty!

In the distance rose the lofty pinnacles, towers, and faint outlines of a vast city; which sparkling in the morning light appeared like alabaster, agate, and pearl, real and yet unreal, like some gorgeous phantasmagoria!

I was taken to this city, where I met Fourier, Shelley, Comte, Mary Wollstonecraft, Mesmer, Hume, Hugh Miller, Buckle, Paine, and many other thinkers of Europe and America. The earnest questioners of immortality while on earth, the humanitarians, and socialistic reformers, I found here associated. They dwell in an Arcadian community, amidst flowers and fountains and cultivated fields, each adding his quota of work and knowledge to the whole.

I attended an entertainment held in a temple fashioned after a Greek model, adorned with paintings and statuary, and heard strains from an orchestra composed of the various instruments of music which have been constructed in all ages of the world! Ravishing sounds filled my ear! It might truly be called the "music of the spheres."

The surprise which attended my entrance in this remarkable world has been so overwhelming that I feel scarcely able to do justice to the subject, and can only hope to give a faint idea of the happiness I have realised in awakening to a second state.

My literary habits and ailments of body induced me to seek a retired life on earth. At Ambleside I was pleased to see my friends and entertain my chosen associates, but I loved the seclusion of a country life and the quiet of my own study, and avoided general society and the excitements of travel; but since I have entered the Spirit-world I have gladly resigned my habits of seclusion. Blest with renewed life and vigour, I have accompanied my spirit-friends on many pleasant and instructive excursions.

Those of my friends who once looked upon me as lost through my Infidelity, have naturally been assiduous in showing me the advantages and beauties of this eternal home! Among these I will name Miss Brontë, Dickens, Mrs. Gaskill, Robert Chambers, and Wordsworth, who were genuinely thankful to the good Lord for permitting my doubting mind to taste the glories of this supernal state.

It were a tedious task to mention all the persons whom I have seen and conversed with; my old anti-slavery confederates hastened to welcome me to this land of freedom; but space and time constrain me to forego entering into further personal details.

The Spirit-world, I am told, is many times larger than earth, and its cities are much more numerous and extensive.

Many kind friends, who have felt grateful for my public efforts to aid the poor working classes of England, have joined together in erecting a dwelling for me here. It is in a very beautiful locality known as the Victoria Garden Home, and is surrounded by a few acres of land. Prince Albert is one of the founders of this community. The site is very fine, and the land undulating and charmingly diversified.

Each homestead is endowed with numerous acres of land, more or less according to the occupant's ability to cultivate them. The party holding one of these domains is expected yearly to look after the comfort and happiness of from six to eight homeless and hapless souls who may make their exit from earth during each year.

You will naturally inquire how Prince Albert became possessed of this estate, since a prince on entering the Spirit-world assumes no higher position than the humblest labouring man? It is true that his birth gave him no prerogative, but his efforts in behalf of the Queen's subjects, and the advancement and sympathy he gave to the fine arts and literature (instead of passing his time in idle pleasure, as too many princes do), raised for him in spirit-life a *coterie* of intelligent minds who determined to make him their leader.

The land chosen was unoccupied, the founders planted and embellished it in much the same manner that land on earth is beautified and made fruitful; and formed it into a " Garden Home."

The soil of the spirit-globe is of a greater depth of alluvial compound than that of your planet, and deposits of slate and stone are rare. Its chemical constituents differ materially from those of earth, and the growth of vegetation is stimulated by the peculiar magnetic condition of our air to a degree unknown to the agriculturists of your world : so much so that mediums, in describing our products, frequently assert that they are produced by a mere effort of the mind, so miraculously rapid is their growth.

The residences are of various styles of architecture, but the Oriental and Grecian types prevail. Those persons who have brought with them a love for any particular homestead, or villa, have erected *fac-similes* of the same, but in most cases the designs are new, and adapted to the salubrious climate with which we are blest.

But the crowning glory of the place is a magnificent temple, grand in proportions and harmonious in design, which rises upon a commanding eminence, like Jove upon Mount Olympus; in it the great, and wise, and good congregate, and send forth their inspirations to humanity, even as the gods did in the fabled ages of the world. In this temple we meet, converse, and study as students did in the golden days of Athens.

Here I have seen assembled many of England's greatest minds—Byron, Scott, Shelley, Mrs. Browning, Coleridge, Charles Lamb, Leigh Hunt ; also Mesmer, Fourier, Faraday, Reichenbach, and hosts of agitators, statesmen, and poets, who have passed away from the old world dissatisfied with life and restless in their aims for a higher condition of humanity, and who live here a happier and more harmonious life.

Here, too, I have met painters,—Reynolds, Haydon, Blake, and Turner ; also the sculptors, Canova, Powers, and Thorwaldsen ; and here, also, at stated times, convene the more advanced minds who have attained to a higher state of existence.

There is one peculiarity which I have observed in spirit-life : that is, spirits avoid living for any long period of time in one place. As a consequence, they interchange visits with neighbouring communities, and organise settlements among spirits of a different nation and language.

Spirits carry with them into the Next World their own peculiarities of dialect (for memory is strengthened by death), but I cannot enter into the minutiæ of their mode of living, and forms of speech, for it would involve subjects which would fill a volume; but I will say that what is known as the socialistic science of life prevails here.

When England's good sovereign, Queen Victoria, leaves her earthly sphere of existence, she will find a lovely home prepared for her by Prince Albert, in this VICTORIA HOME. As I have stated, there is no homage paid to rank here, only to worth. Victoria has ever shown an appreciation of that spiritual fact. She is opposed to false pomp and unnecessary show, and is fitted, beyond any sovereign on earth, to enter into the full enjoyment of spirit-life.

Hoping that the industrious poor and intelligent artisans of earth may speedily understand the advantages of association and co-operation, I close my sketch of " Life in the Spirit-World."

REFORM IN SPIRIT-LIFE.

CHARLES KINGSLEY.

WE were anxious to have an interview with the author of "Alton Locke," of whom we had heard so often. He came, accompanied by a party of friends. His spirit wore a noble, beneficent air, and he spoke with deep feeling upon the subject of the condition of criminals in the other world; his thoughts appeared too overwhelming for his utterance, and it was with difficulty that he conveyed his exalted sentiments through the medium. Having entered upon a world somewhat different from his preconception, and far surpassing it in its limitless variety, he could not find human words to convey the thoughts that pressed upon his spirit. In accordance with the philanthropic feelings that actuated him on earth, he expressed more interest in the condition of the immense number of depraved and ignorant spirits that flock to the shores of the next world, than in that of those more happily situated.

I HAVE ever felt a deep interest in the working classes, and believed that many an humble tailor or shoemaker might, if circumstances favoured advancement, display the wisdom of a Newton, the philanthropy of a Howard, or the bravery of a Nelson.

In my country walks I have often thought I saw "some meek, inglorious Milton" looking out from the dull exterior of a lowly plough-boy, waiting only for the master-stroke of

Fate to reveal his genius. But though I thus believe in an undeveloped ability among the lower classes of England, and think if kindly circumstances had nurtured them, many among them would give forth fruit both good and abundant, yet I have seen a vast number steeped in ignorance and crime, who have inherited evils that no fortunate surroundings could eradicate; and I fear, from facts that have come under my observation, that such on entering the Spirit-world become more fixed in their evils.

It may not be generally known that the earth is surrounded by a belt which to spirits approaching appears like a luminous nebula. It extends just outside the earth's atmosphere, and is the temporary abode of most persons after the decease of the body.

In this stratum of spiritualised earth congregate most of the unfortunate men from your planet who have grown to be drunkards, blacklegs, gamblers, and villains. They congregate in this place, not because they are forced to do so, but from their habits they have no desire to mingle with a better class of society.

I visited this belt soon after my departure from earth. So great is its extent it appears like a world, and every nation has its representative on it. The inhabitants are in close proximity to earth, and it is through them that materialisations and physical manifestations, and all communications of a gross order are given.

On either side of this zone extends a desert, a dreary waste, and hither repair unhappy spirits who desire to elude companionship—wretched beings who have brought their minds to such a mental state, that they prefer to live in this wilderness rather than associate with their fellows. There are very few persons who cannot be touched by the beauties of nature and awakened by the sympathy of a human heart, but there are a few, alas! and they return to earth and give morbid descriptions of their spirit-homes.

Most men are made better by improved conditions, by bright and cheerful surroundings; beautiful objects of form and colour educate men and women into a symmetrical expansion, but the eye must be educated to perceive and the heart to appreciate, before these advantages can be fully enjoyed.

In England many truly noble men have endeavoured in this way to educate the hearts and minds of the lower classes. They have opened parks and built houses of artistic design, to develop the higher instincts of the poor. Factories have also been used for the purpose of manufacturing plates and mugs for the peasantry, embellished with lovely flowers and picturesque scenes, to awaken a love of the beautiful in their overworked minds, and improve their habits generally.

But little can be done at a time; the work of reformation is very slow in those who have inherited depraved appetites and brutish tastes. It takes a lifetime often to break a habit acquired in a few years. It is for this reason that criminals are not immediately benefited in the Spirit-world; though their surroundings may be better, unfortunately, they carry with them their old earth proclivities.

If a man have a love for vice on earth, and encourages that love for a number of years, the mere change of worlds will not bring about a change in his desires and habits.

The time will come when our lawgivers will be better informed on psychological matters, and will cease to send criminals to the Spirit-world by way of punishment; they will grow to understand that offenders can be reformed by being placed in better and healthier conditions on earth. Prisons should be surrounded by acres of tillable land, and hours for recreation and study should be given to the most hardened criminal. It is only by kind treatment that radical reform can be attained; and unless a man can be entirely reformed he will return to earth and instigate his companions in crime to greater evils than he himself had committed: for it is a law that when a spirit becomes disembodied and is free from gross matter, his power increases.

Spirit-life is like a great sea, with many ports, many harbours, and different shores; some beautiful, smiling land, welcoming the voyager, and some barren, desolate shoals and low, rock-bound islands, and some cold dreary coasts, like the coasts of Labrador.

Every man is, happily, created with a life-preserving instinct and a desire to help his fellow. These two principles are the keys to immortality, for no supreme power can save a man from destruction; but his own desire for self-preservation, and the kindly love of spirits whom he may attract will save him from a downward career in the Spirit-world which would be akin to perdition.

How many races of men one meets with in the Spirit-world! What a vast variety of humanity! How great and wise is the arrangement of eternal life—how varied its unending changes of existence! Though we have wished many times that we could write a book informing our fellows of the wonders we have seen, and though erroneous teachings which we have heard given have disheartened us at times, and at other times made us smile, yet we know, in the end you will all reach the same goal, though by different roads, and will all by-and-by breathe the air of these eternal hills.

THE TWO STATES:
THE REAL AND IDEAL.

JUDGE EDMONDS.

THE medium, having read a discourse by Judge Edmonds, delivered through the organism of Mrs. Richmond, inquired of the learned Judge why his description of spirit-life through that talented medium varied from the descriptions conveyed through herself; and while sitting at table received the following communication in answer to her questions.

THE question is asked of me, "How can you harmonise the dissimilar descriptions of the Next World, made by yourself through different mediums? Through one you depict it as a condition objective, and through another as subjective; the one describes it as possessing trees and flowers, hills and dales, rivulets and atmosphere, palaces and cottages, 'things of beauty which are a joy for ever,' and many of the scientific and art appurtenances of earth-life; while at another time, and through another medium, you describe the Spirit-world to be as subjective as are our own dreams, and spirits are described as living in states which their own minds create, similar to the state of an insane person who imagines himself to be a king, and the faded handkerchief or torn hat upon his head to be a crown; while those who are sane behold him as he is, a poor forlorn creature in an insane asylum!

"Spirits, possessed of undue pride, are depicted as building walls of ice wherewith to encase themselves, even as the coral insect builds his precious wall to enclose himself from his enemy; and these walls, states, or conditions are said to vanish or grow according to the advanced or retarded state of the patient!"

My friends and readers, both of these descriptions are correct: one being the *literal* and the other the *ideal* or soul condition of the spirit.

Even in your external world, similar discrepancies in the portrayal of character, places, and things exist. For instance, a religious enthusiast, if asked by an inhabitant of another world to describe himself and your world, would describe himself as living with the Divine Being, as being always in a state of prayer, as having been vile, but by some mysterious process as having been purged by the blood of Christ! Of your beautiful world he would speak with depreciative language, as "a dark, an unwholesome place, a wilderness of sin!" What impression, do you think, would such language convey to the listener?

On the other side, a lover of Nature, like Bryant or Wordsworth, would exult in the beauty of the landscape, speak of the earth as a place of joy, and describe himself as listening to the song of birds, and breathing air perfumed with roses!

The Buddhist absorbed in religious contemplation, never lifts his eye from his sacred book even as he walks, he beholds men pass before him as phantoms, he is in a spiritual opium-dream; so are the pale nuns and austere priests of the Roman Catholic Church. Do they see the earth as you do, think you?

I remember a time, many years ago, during my earth-life, when a certain man, named Miller, asserted that the destruction of the earth would take place at a specified time; many persons became infatuated with the idea, and having implicit belief in his data, awaited the awful moment in a state bordering on insanity. All earthly objects became loathsome in their sight; the houses in which they dwelt, the clothes they wore, and the business they followed became obnoxious and depraved to them, and those who could not believe as they did, were shunned as demons!

How do you think these persons would have described their earthly state to an inhabitant of Jupiter, Mars, or Saturn? Is it possible they could have given a fair judgment of the condition of earth's people?

So with myself, although I endeavour to give a correct account of Spirit-life through the mediums I control, yet my observations are coloured by their mental states, and also by my own mental condition at the time of control.

If I visit the Polar Regions and converse with the Esquimaux, I use comparisons adapted to the climate to which these persons are accustomed, and which they are capable of understanding; and they will be very different from the comparisons I use to an inhabitant of the Tropics.

I have had the happiness of seeing and conversing with Socrates and Plato, Aristotle and Pythagoras, Buddha and Mahomet, Bacon and Voltaire, but how shall I describe to you these interviews? Shall I tell you of the place and moment of occurrence? Shall I tell you how these renowned men were clothed, and how they looked to my eyes? If I do so, you will reply that my description is too material. If I adopt the Oriental typical language, and say, as in the Apocalypse, that they were "clothed with the sun," and that there was "a sound as of a rushing mighty wind" when they spoke, will either mode of speech convey a perfect idea of the fact to your mind?

It is difficult for most mediums to convey a natural impression of the Spirit-world, for they are trammelled by the religious education of themselves and their forefathers. Take an Indian or Chinese, and he will describe the Spirit-world as a world of realities. But the inhabitants of Christendom have so long been taught to look upon the soul as an impalpable nothing, a myth, a flame, something without shape or consistency, an identity capable of feeling the burning of a material hell-fire without being consumed! that they fail to comprehend spirit in its natural condition.

Monks and priests, Churchmen and Dissenters, have taught you to despise the body as an unworthy form, having no kinship to the soul, or likeness thereto. We have been taught that dress, and all the paraphernalia of civilisation are the result of the *Fall*, and therefore must be ignored by a pure and elevated spirit.

People do not recall the fact that all the wonderful machinery of man's design, the appliances of Nature's forces to the production of new results, the fabric of silks, laces, and beautiful objects, are the outcome of man's God-like powers, and that the higher he progresses in development, the more capable he becomes of designing and creating like a very God!

In the Spirit-world man's capabilities increase ten-fold, and the objects he designs increase in proportionate ratio.

I hailed with delight while on earth, this medium through whom I now talk, because I perceived in her the faculty of receiving natural impressions, and discovered that through her, spirits could describe real scenes and places, while through others equally gifted, they could only describe the poetic and vague semblances of facts.

I would have you listen to my words: remember that in the Spirit-world, as on the material earth, there are *two states:* the ideal, visionary one, and the real, materialistic condition, so to speak; and that these states interlink the one with the other; and that mind is ever seeking for an expression of its idea in visible form, in the Spirit-world as in your world; and, as the Creator has formed the millions of objective worlds in the sidereal heavens, and all the natural objects you view on the earth, so you will continue, like Him, to form in Spirit-life objective articles as the result of your creative thought, and live a life as real and objective as the one you now live on earth.

RICH MEN OF NEW YORK.

JUDGE EDMONDS.

Immediately after Vanderbilt's decease, several gentlemen who had known him for years on the Road, desired the friends of the medium to inquire as to his spiritual condition, and in response to this demand for information as to his state, Judge Edmonds controlled the medium, and gave the following account. In the course of his remarks he was apparently interrupted, and the medium could not continue for some time. Upon recommencing, the Judge announced that Vanderbilt had entered the room, and remonstrated with him upon the statements he had made, after which he completed the succeeding account.

HAVE been requested to describe the condition of a few of the noted rich men of New York, and I will, as Othello says,

"Speak of them as they are; nothing extenuate,
Nor set down aught in malice."

It is contrary, to the general purpose of this work, for one man to speak for another; but as it has been permitted me to make my remarks, I will do so as freely as I would if I were discoursing in a lecture-room in New York, and endeavour to point out the evil results of a certain course in life, for the purpose of enlightening my former fellow citizens, not desiring to say anything unkind or derogatory of these gentlemen who, while on earth, were my fellow-townsmen, and who are now residing in the Spirit-world, although in a different quarter from myself.

The City of Spring Garden, where I reside, and the Society of Beulah, of which I am a member (and of which Greeley is president) are not yet likely to prove attractive to such men as Vanderbilt, or A. T. Stewart; but should they desire to visit the city in which I make my home, I will be very happy to greet them.

VANDERBILT.

It has been facetiously remarked of a famous divine, who made converts to Christianity by the score, and by his wonderful eloquence moved the most hardened sinner to tears of repentance—yet in whose life an undercurrent ran quite contrary to his sacred teaching and calling,—it has been said of him that he had opened an oyster saloon in the Spirit-world! This, however, is not the literal fact, the humorous public thus adjusting his punishment to suit his demerits, and while applauding him as an orator, keenly appraising his foibles as a man.

In the like manner, public opinion, deals with the railroad king, VANDERBILT, and sarcastically speculates as to what place of honour his death-bed repentance will give him on the Golden Shore. He has shut the door of his stables on his fast trotters, turned his back on his boon companions, emptied his pockets of his millions, and started alone and on foot, on his solitary journey to an almost unknown world, where men are taken at their true worth, and where extraneous advantages of wealth and power which they have acquired on earth, are utterly valueless.

Yesterday, an oration was poured out over the body of

this whilom rich man, to-day, he is a denizen of the Spirit-world—poor and almost friendless! He will have to commence his life anew, and develop his higher faculties, which have been almost suppressed within him.

Men, in earth-life, take a sort of satisfaction in believing that in the next, justice will be meted out, and that the poor man will become rich, and the rich man poor, and that those now in power will sit at the feet of those who now abjectly bow before them. In one sense this is a correct view of what takes place. Every man is there the possessor of what he has acquired on earth, mentally and morally, be it good or bad.

Vanderbilt's mental development to acquire and over-reach, would, in the Spirit-world, place him with the lowest of the low if he did not posses some other aspiring intuitions which will save him from companionship of that sort. I met him when he arrived here; his mother and some friends joined him, but he looked disappointed and broken when they led him away to their quiet and humble home. His life here for a time will be one of severe training. He can no longer handle his millions, and control and force men to yield to him the lion's share.

It was not pleasant to see the crowd of spirits—victims of the Astabula disaster, who confronted Vanderbilt, and poured out their censures upon him, for not applying a small portion of his immense wealth towards making his road safe from disaster and accident, by every appliance of art and invention.

There is no excuse for negligence, carelessness, want of supervision, and bad bridges, excepting poverty. Lack of sleep and food may make a man negligent; lack of good engineering skill may cause a bridge to break away by force of tide, or undue weight upon it; but when the President of such a road is the owner of millions of money, the best engineers in the world are at his command. His employés should be so well paid that want of rest and lack of food should never serve as excuses for accidents. If a premium were offered for the best constructed bridges, and human life were held as precious as money, we would not have so many unwilling guests hastily ushered into Spirit-life.

Until man learns to deal justly with his fellow-men, he cannot be happy in the Spirit-world.

All the present schemes of trade and commerce are wrong. The means by which one man obtains wealth and holds control of the market, and over-rides and oppresses his neighbour, are wrong; such practices are not permitted in the Spirit-world, and the person who takes pleasure in that sort of life finds his occupation gone when he reaches our spirit-planet.   *   *   *   *   *

I am sorry to say that Vanderbilt's religious impressions were not very well grounded. Nourished in the hotbed of a sick-room, they had but a mushroom existence and have already come to an untimely end. He was heard to swear soon after his arrival, and curse his minister for not giving him a truer idea of heaven.

Habits of a long life are not changed by the sudden translation from earth to a spiritual sphere. Three days ago I spoke to you of his arrival in Spirit-life; he is back to earth already, seeking to undo his WILL and add new bequests. He walks around the house and stables he once possessed, vainly endeavouring to make his friends see and hear him, and is beginning to realise that death is not that *quiet rest* in the arms of a Crucified Redeemer, which from the teachings that were given him in his hours of weakness he supposed it to be!

I am happy to say his endeavours may not prove futile,

and that his efforts to remedy his mistakes are likely to produce some beneficial result from the large fortune he left behind him.*

Vanderbilt was eminently a man of intuitions, and if left to Nature, would have had correct ideas of Spirit-life. However, the artificial and false views of heaven in vogue among Christians, choked up any common-sense opinions he may have formed, and turned his thoughts and hopes in an erratic channel. He was well aware of spiritual manifestations on earth, but unfortunately his communications were not of a high order and were directed towards acquiring material wealth. And here I must raise my voice against a gross mis-application of mediumship. It is true that a class of spirits of low type exist in the Spirit-world. There are there vast crowds of uneducated men of every race on earth: blacklegs, gamblers, and sensualists of the lowest type, who are only too happy to control a medium and disseminate their vicious ideas.

I regret to say that the rich men of New York take a lower position in Spirit-life than many of the wealthy noblemen of England. America, which has been the refuge of the poor and oppressed of other countries, should awaken in the hearts of all who have made immense fortunes on her protecting shores, a desire to assist homeless wanderers,—sons of toil and poverty, who might be aided spiritually and materially by a wise distribution of a portion of the great wealth they have accumulated.

Rich men who have failed on earth to lay up treasures in heaven, in the Spirit-world are poor vagrants, subsisting on the charity of kind spirits, who on earth have once been humble porters and poor clerks to those very individuals.

---

* Given previous to his will being contested.

A. T. STEWART

Is more pleasantly situated here. He had created for himself many friends in Spirit-life by his efforts to improve the condition of the working-women, and to build cheap and desirable homes for mechanics, clerks, and industrious men. His views of business life were strict and hard, but he justly considered idleness the bane of existence; and a want of systematic industry as the cause of most of the miseries of life; and in this opinion he was correct; but the good he might have done he left undone. Every man should consider himself a steward for invisible angels and should so dispose of his accumulations that they would benefit humanity.

ASTOR

Spends much of his time in Germany and America; he is happily situated and doing much good. He often visits his friend Washington Irving and is reaping the benefits of the library which he founded, as no doubt Vanderbilt will in future time receive advantages from the college which he endowed.

You know the New Testament says, "Make to yourselves friends of the mammon of unrighteousness; that, when ye fail, they may receive you into everlasting habitations." This is true, the more friends one makes and retains on earth, the better off is that person when he becomes a denizen of our immortal world. Jesus taught this truth to his disciples. He was a medium and a clairvoyant, and was perfectly familiar with the truths I am telling you, with which I wish every rich and poor man of New York would become practically acquainted.

IMMORTALITY.

JOHN STUART MILL.

WE had assembled in our sitting-room, not knowing who, from among the names we had selected to contribute to our new book, would accept our invitation that evening, when the medium fell into a trance, and John Stuart Mill, whom we had overlooked in our invitations, appeared, and spoke with earnestness in the following eloquent strain. He seemed overwhelmed with the wonders of the Next World, and filled the mind of the clairvoyant with stupendous questions. Happy in his new-found life, the double feeling of joy in his discovery, and sadness that he should have groped on earth so long in darkness, pervaded his discourse.

Y life on earth was clouded by doubt: science and the forces of Nature alike seemed to drive me to the conclusion that man had not an immortal soul.

I looked at Nature. The flowers sprang up and died; trees grew up slowly and battled for years with the elements, and they in turn died, and that was the end of them. Animals followed in the footsteps of vegetation: the quiet sheep grazed their few peaceful days, and they also were converted into food and passed from sight for ever. So with man's companions the horse and the dog, after serving their masters a few dutiful years, they too were carted off as refuse, to return no more.

I looked at man and sought to read in his life the superintending guidance of some Invisible Power, but in its place I found a material force thrusting down the weak, the greater overpowering the lesser, and no divine aid adjusting these evils. I stretched my hands up to the sky, I surveyed the heavens with the telescope, and there, where in our imagination, in our poetic dreams, we had placed spirits, I found material worlds. Even the stars were not what they seemed; those bright luminaries which awakened in the mind vague and undefined feelings of immortality, when viewed by the eye of science through the mighty lens of man's invention, proved to be material earths like our own—matter whirling through space propelled by the same force that propels our own planet, and that force not even, as we supposed, nor as we had been taught by theologians to believe it to be, "the hand of God holding them in space," but the result of combinations, simple and easily understood—the laws of attraction and gravitation !

I say that I failed to find any proof of immortality on earth.

Man grew up like the tree, waxed old, and died. Apparently he went the "way of all the earth;" if he possessed an immortal soul, it was unseen at the death of the body. When I studied the science of development and saw that the survival of the fittest was the rule, and the good man was carried off not because he was good but because he was weak, and that no Providence nor spiritual power could prevent this result,—when I discovered this I became hopeless; my heart was saddened and discouraged, life seemed scarcely worth the struggle with the untoward events which confronted it.

But when I closed my eyes on this world's disappointments, vexations, and doubts, and opened them in another—

a World of Spirits—the load left me, the weight was taken from my heart, doubts and sadness vanished. It seemed so natural to revive, to live again, that I marvelled I should ever have doubted man's immortality; and, on finding him not a god, not a seraph, but merely a refined form of materiality, the enigma that puzzled me on earth was solved.

The Universal Creators of mankind, of the inhabitants of suns and systems that wheel through space in innumerable numbers, these Creators, I repeat, are to me invisible. I know not their parts nor properties, but I know this, they have given the undying principle of progression to man, they have stamped it upon his spirit and rendered him immortal.

I will not speak of the character of this Spirit-world—of its material aspects—others can describe it better than I can, but I will tell you that every dwarfed aspiration of the human soul has here a chance to expand and blossom, that the physically strong, who by mere brute force triumph on earth, are here weak and powerless, and it is the mental and spiritual nature of man that is pre-eminent.

To the poor and honest peasantry of England who bear with patience in a hopeful spirit their lot, I would say that they have here better homes and more honourable positions, than those who would oppress and subjugate them.

HOME OF HORACE GREELEY.

HORACE GREELEY.

Mr. G——, a gentleman formerly interested in the Anti-Slavery cause and an earnest advocate of Communism, having called and introduced himself as being especially interested in "Strange Visitors," and pleased to learn of the natural condition of the Next World, the conversation turned upon Horace Greeley, the great American journalist and advocate of land reform; and upon Mr. G—— desiring to obtain Mr. Greeley's views of Communism in the Spirit-world the medium was controlled, and Mr. Greeley spoke as follows :—

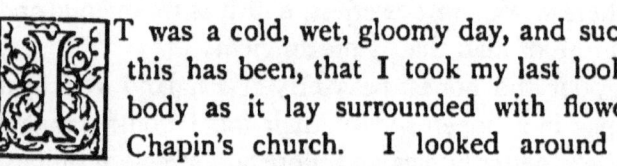

IT was a cold, wet, gloomy day, and such a one as this has been, that I took my last look upon my body as it lay surrounded with flowers in Dr. Chapin's church. I looked around upon the multitude convened in that building, and recognised many an old friend—nay, I touched them, and proffered my hand for a last farewell! They perceived me not; their eyes were fixed upon the lifeless form; the spirit-body they could not see! I knew that I was invisible to them, for I was not ignorant of the spiritual philosophy; although externally I rejected it, mentally I accepted it as a truth.

I was glad to be free from the body, for during that fearful presidential campaign I had been influenced by many conflicting minds, and been forced to subscribe to policies and actions to which I was opposed. Harassed, and wearied, disappointed in my prospects, and humiliated by friends who should have sustained me, I longed to escape from earth, the more so that I no longer retained my usual judgment; like a lion with his foot in a net, the more I endeavoured to extricate myself, the more I became involved in its meshes. I looked around upon that crowd as it dispersed, and realised that I was free. There was nothing to hold me to earth longer, and, accompanied by a few friends, I set off on my first voyage to the World of Spirits.

The atmosphere was heavy, and we made our way through it with difficulty. We did not go straight upward, as I had imagined we should do, but took a northerly direction over the city, stopping at Chappaqua* to satisfy my desire to take a last look of my farm before I departed, and to see some of my improvements. Tears of emotion filled my eyes when I walked around the old house, viewed the ground I had improved, crossed the little bridge, and stood upon my favourite knoll, with hair streaming in the air; then I realised I could not again with my physical form plant, and contrive, and beautify that old farm. Margaret Fuller was one of the party accompanying me; she was always fond of the woods, and, finding that I was overcome by my feelings, she urged me to proceed on my journey.

It was with a sensation of relief that we turned off into a pathway of light, though it was, in truth, more like a broad river than a pathway. A cool, balmy stratum of air, like that of our home woods in summer-time, pervaded the road. We pursued our way with increasing velocity, for, I should think, the space of fifteen or twenty minutes, passing through what is known as the stellar region, which astronomers tell us is a cold, dark void, and which, to mortal sensations, would

---

* The Indian name of the village where Greeley resided.

be colder than the polar regions, but which I found to be
favoured with this soft, spring-like air, caused by the electrical
current, which, like the gulf-stream, flowed directly through
this region.

I have since traversed this open space in a shorter time,
but, in this my first voyage, I think it was fully fifteen minutes
before I caught sight of any habitation or life, when suddenly
I seemed to see land stretching out below me—mountains,
rivers, and distant foliage, as a balloonist sees spread beneath
his gaze the face of Nature while descending from his voyage
among the clouds.

We sailed for a considerable time over a beautiful country,
—I following the guidance of my friends, who were steering
for some familiar quarter where we were expected. I noticed
that portions of the land over which we passed were uncultivated, and bore a general resemblance to the earth which
I had just left.

Presently we began to make our descent to a tower
situated upon a hill, which on reaching I found to be a light,
beautiful structure of a composite style of architecture. It
stood upon an extensive plot of ground embracing several
acres, beautified by flowers and ornamental shrubs, and was,
in fact, what you would call on earth an hotel or depôt. We
landed on one of the balconies, and entered through a porch
to the inner part of the building.

The floors of this ante-room were covered with a species
of silk matting embroidered in handsome designs representing welcome and greeting to friends. I took especial notice
of this covering or carpet, as it was to me a new fabric.
The walls were hung with mirrors, which very much resembled those I had seen on earth, and, looking in one, I
saw myself reflected, appearing about thirty years younger,
but still natural to my memory of myself.

We passed on; a door leading to an adjoining room was opened, and I was immediately met by a crowd of friends, foremost among whom were Henry Clay and Abraham Lincoln. A host of literary men, whom I had known in my position as journalist for the last twenty years of my life, gathered about me: many men who had disappeared from earth in the memorable battles between the North and South. Among those whom I personally knew I discovered General Scott; also Richardson, whose tragic fate lives in the memory of many.

It is almost impossible to describe my feelings as I saw so many familiar faces which had passed out of my mind, it had seemed to me, for ever!

And how did these people appear? you may ask. Did they really look like men you meet every day on the streets or on 'Change. I could detect no essential difference, excepting that they appeared more youthful and less careworn.

After talking for a while about the political condition of the United States, and of the nomination of General Grant, whom I found they all upheld pretty strongly, "Well, President Greeley," said my old friend Abraham Lincoln, in his jocose manner; "as we could not make you President of the United States, we will make you President of our Agricultural Society, and chief officer of a community which will be more in harmony with your views and development than occupancy of the White House would have been."

They then proposed to take me to see this agricultural community. I acquiesced in the proposition, and we went out of the building, descending a magnificent stairway, constructed of a variety of stone of a pale saffron colour. Upon my remarking the peculiar beauty and polish of this stone, one of the company informed me that it was a mere composition, and that the principles of Nature were so well understood in the Spirit-world that almost any gem or marble could be imitated by spirits.

On either side of the broad steps, upon massive pedestals, stood an immense globe: one surmounted by a phœnix-like bird, the other by a ship artistically designed,—the one representing the spiritual, and the other the material world. A long avenue, proceeding from this entrance and extending to the gates, was paved through the centre with a similar highly polished composition inlaid in allegorical designs, with colours of pale violet and rose. On either side of this avenue grew trees of a light, feathery foliage, whose arching branches met and formed a beautiful canopy over the path.

At regular distances down this broad road were placed figures raised on pedestals, representing the native animals of America. I examined everything carefully. On each side of this path, beyond these carved images, were beds composed of a short, purple kind of grass. These pastures were adorned with magnificent fountains. A group of marble swans formed the base of one, and the water poured from their several beaks; in the centre above them rose a species of colossal ostrich, its head and neck stretched high up in the air, throwing forth volumes of water to an immense height. Another devise was composed of flowers; mammoth pond lilies, with intertwined leaves, formed the base, while a graceful variety of the pitcher plant made the central column, the water gushing from the uplifted calyx.

I was very much diverted by these extraordinary fountains, and the constant flow of water both surprised and delighted me, as I had never thought of the probability of seeing water in a spiritual locality.

On reaching the gates we found a pretty little open carriage awaiting us; it was lined with a white crapey material, embossed with golden flowers. This carriage moved by a mechanical contrivance which I will not now describe, an electric force carried it over the ground as smoothly as would a pair of horses. The road was fine, and the face of the country fresh, green and agreeable to the eye. The spiritual sun was shining brightly, while the thermometer stood, I should say, at about eighty or ninety, a most pleasant breeze fanning us at the time. The air was refreshingly fragrant, more so than any field of new-mown hay I had ever smelt on earth.

About an hour's drive over this magnificent road brought us to our destination. Here we alighted; our party consisting of Henry Clay, Daniel Webster, A. Lincoln, and myself, each an ardent lover of farming, and with pleasant congratulations they introduced me to my farm.

We entered through an open gateway, and proceeded up to a house. I could scarcely believe my eyes, it seemed my old place at Chappaqua over again! The ground was the same; some of my very improvements appeared before me. "How under the sun is this?" said I to Henry Clay, "this seems Chappaqua reproduced!"

"Part of it is the work of your friends and part of it your own effort. Many times when you thought you were in your own bed dreaming of improvements you intended making on your farm, you were actually working here. A number of years before you left earth, you, no doubt, noticed how abstracted you became; it grew daily more difficult to arouse you to your former state of activity. Well, that condition was owing to the fact that your spirit was here, busy preparing itself a home before its arrival."

This struck me as a remarkable statement. *Here*, it seems, like a somnambulist, I had been walking and working in my sleep! "Do other people do the same?" I asked.

"To be sure, many do; and if mankind were only aware of this ability, they would work more intelligently and produce better results." "For years and years on earth," said Lincoln, "you have been advocating the doctrine that the able and energetic youths should leave the crowded cities and 'go west.' Well, those among the young men who were industrious and worthy, and cut off from life by the accidents of war and disease, were brought to this association in your name; we have denominated it *The Greeley Happy Home* Association. It is an odd name, but an appropriate one, as every hour spent here is a happy one. Those who prefer call it by its more poetic one of "*Beulah.*'" He then showed me around the grounds.

Before I enter into a detailed description of the place, I must premise something about the climate of this favoured land. Our climate is much more equable than that of earth, owing to local causes, our peculiar revolution around our sun and magnetic and electrical influences which predominate. Some of the cereals raised on earth are not cultivated here; others unknown to you take their place. We have not the large animal creation to supply with food that you possess. Flesh is not at all used in the Spirit-world as an article of diet; we live on fruit, &c. Natural scenery here is so similar to that of earth, that one expects to find a similarity in all points; but there is a radical difference.

I found that the association comprised about ten thousand acres of land, and numbered over a hundred dwellings: beautiful rural places, each park or ground containing a fountain; a broad stream running through a portion of the estate, and handsome bridges spanning it at regular distances.

The working element of this community is composed largely of young men, who, in this agreeable home, follow one of the noblest pursuits which man is capable of engaging in. The system by which these persons are introduced to the community and given occupation, is the following admirable one :—

A certain number of individuals are selected from the society from time to time, and to them is assigned the duty of visiting earth, and studying the character and life of any party to whom they may be attracted, or, of whom they may accidentally hear, with a view to their eligibility as members; and if, in the judgment of the band, it is considered wise to assign a future place to the person in the society of "Happy Homes," a portion of land is set apart for him or her, and a dwelling or materials for a dwelling appropriated for their use. At the moment of their departure from earth, they are met and escorted to their homes here, and directly become actively engaged. They are so well pleased that they cannot be persuaded to leave the community.

As for myself, although I have been here but a short time, I would not willingly change places with anyone that I know of. I have both occupation and leisure. Besides the business of superintending this society, I am engaged in editing a spiritual paper, as I found it impossible to resign my old habits and occupations; therefore, to satisfy the demands of friends, the needs of society, and my own inclinations, I have assumed the editorship of *The Spiritual Tribune*. I have, as you perceive, adhered to the old favourite name. It is published in the city of Spring-Garden, about sixteen miles from my community home.

Not long before I took up my residence here, two very dear friends of mine came to reside in this place. They are talented and earnest women, and well known in the literary world for their pure, sweet poems. When it was understood in the Spirit-world that they were soon to leave earth, a pretty residence was constructed for them, on a retired portion of these grounds, by friends who were familiar with their tastes and requirements.

Each friend and admirer contributed some useful gift and thus the little dwelling was furnished. A choice library was formed by many friends presenting books. Some lady artist made a gift of beautiful spirit-dishes, more elegant than Sevres china, I am told, transparent as a spider's web, and decorated in lovely colours—the whole their own design and manufacture. The balconies and porticos of the dwelling were adorned with flowering plants, and, when all was complete, friends who had been attending on these sisters—Alice and Phœbe Cary—brought one alone from earth to her beautiful home.

Beautiful though it was, to her it was desolate; she pined for her sister, her friend and companion of so many years. She could not rest satisfied; it was impossible to divert her mind. Her yearning was so strong, her agony at the separation so intense, that it was felt by the lonely sister in her remote home away on earth, so that she drooped and withered away, and ere long these two, who had passed so many years together in life, were re-united in the Spirit-world.

One of my greatest pleasures is to visit their pretty cottage. I find in them womanly sympathy and interest in every noble and useful project. Their poetic aspirations inspire me with happiness.

I give their case as an example of how those who are worthy are situated in the Spirit-world.

I wish to say a few words about the handsome monumen which my brothers and co-labourers in the art of printing have erected to my memory. I am overwhelmed with emotion when I reflect on the tribute they have paid to one who wishes he were more worthy of their noble deed.

I attended the unveiling at Greenwood. I not alone, but in company with some thousands of spirits. I stood above the knoll, looking toward the sea—a spirit unseen—and listened to the words that fell from the lips of the speaker (Bayard Taylor). I had the satisfaction to remember that I had assisted him in his early career. I hope that monument may inspire those who may take my place on earth to lend a helping hand to those who are struggling with life and its difficulties.

I wish that bronze head could speak to the young men who crowd your great cities, and tell them to go home to their farms, to their father's homesteads, or otherwise to strike out, like bold pioneers, into the Far West, and there, with their own right hands, build homes for themselves and families.

If your government would aid your young men to open up and settle the wilderness, and would take the money that they now spend in fighting the Indians, and other unholy causes, and expend it on the bone and sinew of the country, you would find that ere long, America would bloom like a second Paradise; that want and crime would diminish in your fair land.

I wish what I say would reach through the length and breadth of our country, and that those who despair on earth and are atheistic, and have doubt of a future state, would learn from me that the Spirit-world is a world of beauty and use, and that all knowledge they obtain on earth, will be more than profitable to them hereafter.

EVOLUTION.

PROF. AGASSIZ.

When Prof. Agassiz spoke through the medium, the favourite theory of Evolution was being propounded by the scientific world. One of the learned English advocates of this theme had just visited the shores of the New World, and the American clergy were trembling before the new theory, and from every pulpit of the land, discourses were thundered in an effort to make the discoveries of Science conform to the traditions of the Christian Bible, and to our astonishment, the Professor gave forth the following rather startling account of our origin.

I COME from my island home at the call of science, hoping to add something to the information already obtained.

This lady, blindfolded and mesmerised, is rendered sensitive to invisible forces, and in this condition her soul is capable of travelling through space, and taking cognizance of strange unaccredited facts that are transpiring outside of this terrestrial plane of existence.

When restored to her natural condition, the knowledge thus obtained appears to her vague and indistinct, and even while entranced it is difficult for her to perfectly describe what she sees, or to repeat with adequate language what is told her.

This condition of affairs must be borne in mind by my reader in endeavouring to understand the subject of which I treat.

It is but recently that science has been able to trace the record of your globe and the inhabitants thereof; you perceive therefore, if it is difficult to obtain a knowledge of the world on which you live, it must be infinitely more difficult to obtain information of a region so remote as the world which I inhabit.

Geologists will tell you of mammoth animals that lived on the earth centuries ago, and from the beds of rivers dried up and silent for ever, they gather the mighty fragments and fossilised bones of the fauna of a by-gone geological period, and articulate those immense carcases so that they stand before the spectator, strange, inconceivable forms, repulsive and demon-like to the eye unfamiliar with such creations, while they were familiar enough to the beings who lived coeval with their existence. As on your world there have been beings who would appear grotesque and almost impossible creations to the eye of to-day, so on every earth there has been a series of similar evolutions prior to man's taking up his abode thereon.

Man being the perfection of animal form (whose origin is the source of acute investigation by archæologists and geologists), whose moral and mental faculties place him far above the lower animals, causes a break in the development theory which puzzles the astutest mind of the New School.

My investigations since I have become an inhabitant of this superior world have satisfied me that man originally migrated to earth from a superior planet.

Of his migratory character and the tendency of a higher

race to assimilate and fraternise with a lower one, you have a corroborative truth in the rise and fall of nations on earth with their attendant results.

At a remote period this globe was surrounded by an atmosphere very different from that of to-day, and the present race of men could not have existed. During this period to which I allude, earth was visited by beings from a spirit-world, drawn hither by a force of magnetic attraction, which then was a powerful agent, of whose force science gives but a faint idea to the student of Nature.

Influenced by this force, and the spirit of adventure, and by the migratory habit which is co-existent with Nature, this colony of spirits visited your earth. They were men and women of giant-like structure, and they settled on a portion of land which was submerged through the subsequent convulsions of Nature.

The offspring of these beings deteriorated in size, and became more material than their parents by a process of acclimatisation. As I have stated, it was owing to a peculiar condition of earth and atmosphere, that these spiritual beings were able to take up a physical abode upon the earth. In order to understand this statement of fact, the reader must bear in mind that what is called spiritual and immaterial is merely a refined attribute of matter. That electricity, magnetism, and the Od force are the components of spirit, and are in reality refined material forces, and that spirit and matter are identical, yet differing as heat differs from cold, and light differs from opacity.

These beings, as I term them, were of different grades of perfection. The most highly developed among them brought a taste for music, sculpture, and painting, and a love for beautiful and graceful forms, of which their descendants in ancient Egypt and Greece have left mementos.

As I have said, these beings (who, in the present atmosphere, would be unseen by a mortal's eye upon the earth), drew around them a material covering, and as man now throws off every seven years the outer form, supplying its place with new material, so they gathered to themselves from surrounding elements corporeal forms, which, however, they in time relinquished.

The existence of the first race of men was of a much longer duration than that of the present inhabitants of earth. The physical forms in each succeeding generation, while deteriorating, became less adapted to the necessities of the spirit; and now it is only by the aid of science and the constant application of inventions to the wants of the body, that to-day man's spirit is able to preserve its existence within its present frail tenement.

It is impossible to go back to the origin of life, because it is of eternity; and I believe candidly myself, that there has been no beginning.

I know that there are worlds in existence more numerous than the sands on the sea shore, and an eternity could not number them. These worlds are peopled with beings possessing moral and spiritual powers. They have various degrees of skill and natural ability: some superior to those of the inhabitants of earth, and others inferior. These beings live on for ever in different degrees of sublimation; and as the winged seed which is borne along the air bears its fructifying life to a distant soil, so in the superior world spiritual inhabitants are carried by magnetic and electric forces to people distant worlds.

The comet, that strange visitant, carries in its brilliant flying chariot, spirits on the same mission through space.

I apprehend that what now seems obscure to scientists will be deciphered and made clear by future investigations in the science of magnetism and Spiritualism. From my home here above the clouds, on this beautiful island where I pursue my studies, I watch with deep interest the investigations of such men as Wallace, Tyndall, Crookes, Lubbock, and the large *coterie* of English students, and their brethren in America and in other parts of the world.

STATESMANSHIP
FROM A SPIRITUAL STANDPOINT.

SECRETARY SEWARD.

THE difficult problem of reconstructing the southern portion of the American States having engaged the profoundest thoughts of the Executive (President Grant) for eight years with but indifferent success, and the distinguished Secretary of State having been familiar with the producing causes of the existing inharmony, it was thought that his knowledge of mundane affairs from his present position would be both interesting and valuable. Hence his views and those of his present associates were requested, and are here recorded. They will be read with solicitude, as the new policy of the present Executive (President Hayes) is now being applied.

ELEASED from the cares of State at Washington, I shook off my time-worn body, but had no sooner set my foot on this immortal soil, than I heard that I had received an appointment in the Spiritual Capitol of the United States, and on its being shown that it was my duty to accept the mission, I accordingly acquiesced.

I find that this world is the old world duplicated and enlarged, though composed of rather better material, like a new and improved edition of an old book,—your world corresponding to the old "Fust" type, and ours to the best, clear-faced metallic type of modern printers.

Everything, I say, is duplicated. The United States with its capitals; also Europe, Africa, and Asia: even I, myself am a duplicate of a former Seward who lived and died in America. As you may remember, I had just completed my voyage around the world, when health failed me, and I was obliged to close the door of my mortal house for ever.

That last voyage so interested and instructed me, that I determined to make a similar one, during the summer, around the world that I now inhabit; and though this earth is many times larger than yours, I accomplished the trip in a much less space of time than is required to traverse yours.

An overland journey is impossible on your earth, as the connecting land-links are gone. The convulsions of Nature that have broken up your land into islands, and separated the great continents, have not apparently taken effect in this sphere.

The Pacific and Atlantic Oceans have here dwindled into comparatively small lakes, consequently the extent of territory is much greater on our side than on yours.

Before I came to this Summer-land, I used to entertain an idea that people lived everywhere and nowhere when they became spirits.

The statement made in the Bible that there should be "one tongue and one people," I presume led me to think this. But you are fast approaching to that state of the millennium in America, where the German, French, Italian, Dane, Swede, and African, all live on an equal footing, and make themselves understood by the same language, and yet retain a partiality for their mother tongue.

The long stretch of land from the Eastern States to California is much more thickly settled in the Spirit-world, than on earth.

Thriving cities exist with us where there is but a nucleus at present with you.

The large army of men who were cut off during the late war have added greatly to the population of that region.

Passing through California, and journeying to China and Japan, I found those countries in a high state of civilisation, holding very friendly relations with our own country, anxious to disseminate knowledge and grant equal rights and advantages to all.

But everywhere peculiarities of race still exist,—the Hindoos and Turks each retaining their particular marks of character, colour, and development, though possessing less arbitrary forms of government; and civilisation proceeds in the Spirit-world pretty much as it does on earth.

Mahomet and Confucius have both their followers in this world, as men, mortal or immortal, seem bound to follow some ideal teacher.

I forgot to state that the city of Jerusalem, which I visited, is almost a *fac-simile* of the Jerusalem described in the New Testament.

It is a very ancient city, and is built with all the luxuriousness of Oriental design, rather like the ancient Nineveh, some of the streets being literally paved with gold (gold being very abundant in the Spirit-world, yet even there it is considered a precious metal).

It is especially noticeable that this world in its general aspects resembles the natural world, but in its minutiæ it widely differs. Countless industries are carried on here, and to the multiplicity of inventions there seems no end.

The comparatively modern inventions of communicating by telegraph, by the magnetic battery, and by the vibrations of the human voice conveying thought to great distances by means similar to the telephone, have long been known in the Spirit-world, and practised there.

Most of the industries and inventions peculiar to spirits are unknown to the inhabitants of the earth as yet, and I can merely allude to the fact of our possessing such, without describing them.

I have been very much gratified with my experience here so far, and must add my testimony to that of others by saying that the second stage of existence is perfectly in consonance with man's spiritual aspirations and development When I say spiritual, I mean his intellectual as well as moral characteristics.

One peculiarity of this state is its juxtaposition to earth, and the constant intercourse which is kept up between the two worlds induces a ceaseless travelling back and forth.

I have been greatly astonished, as all newly arrived have been, to see the vast floating population that hang around the earth like parasites, who live unseen, in and among certain classes of mankind.

Advanced spirits are continually developing new plans for the improvement and guardianship of this class, yet many elude our supervision, and cause great disturbances on earth.

From my remarks you will perceive that we do not live in a state of perfection, but benevolent schemes for the improvement and benefit of such uneducated spirits are constantly being planned, and statesmen devise methods to adjust differences that arise between the educated and uneducated.

The ignorant portion of the community is almost as numerous in this world as on earth.

I have already stated the fact of my holding office here

(I use this familiar term as being easily comprehended), and I will now briefly allude to the method. We present the anomaly of the existence of three or four generations of men at the same time, and in the same district of country.

For instance, Washington still lives in the spiritual United States, and is the honorary head of the Union in both worlds. We, the younger generation, who have been interested in national affairs, act under his direction, and to me he has delegated the position of attending President Hayes, and of reporting political matters transpiring on earth.

The difficulties that have attended the last political campaign are matters of serious consideration to those in the Spirit-world, who are concerned in the welfare of your nation, and who desire it to be the exponent of the most progressive government, closely allied to the highest spiritual one, which is destined in time to become the universal government of the earth.

A government which affords equal rights to all of its people, which knows neither bond nor free, but a whole people only, one and indissoluble, cannot, in rendering assistance to one section, forego its duty to the other.

The State may be likened to the human body with its various members, one of which being disabled by a wound or sore, the first duty would be to restore, if possible, the disabled member to a state of health.

Thus several good conscientious men, of whom Abraham Lincoln is foremost, have sanctioned the policy adopted by President Hayes of soothing the fever in the sick member (what is called "humouring it" for the time being, while it is in a state of distress), which it is hoped will prove the means of restoring it to perfect health.

It remains to be seen if this policy be the correct one.

Among the enlightened, kindness is a sure means to produce friendship, but with the ignorant and undeveloped, kindness is often mistaken for cowardice, and evil advantage is taken of leniency.

I would advise a middle course. Let us endeavour to conciliate the South, but warily, and then let Northern men pour into that section of country. Let them educate the blacks and start the wheels of commerce, teaching them that industry, and not idleness, is the great source of happiness here as hereafter.

METEMPSYCHOSIS.

BULWER (LORD LYTTON).

WHILST Bulwer was controlling the medium she felt as though sailing over a summer sea; a delicious dreamy langour stole over her senses, and she spoke as though entranced by golden memories. The subject of re-incarnation had evidently interested the mind of the author as it has many Spiritualists

and find that the celebrated Italian lakes and islands are evidently the reflex of heavenly ones.

The soul, while still controlling the body, has evidently the wondrous power of migrating from point to point in God's great universe.

The doctrine of Metempsychosis was a favourite one of mine. I delighted to revel in the idea that the soul of Petrarch, or Tasso, or some ancient Greek lyrist, was revisiting the earth, and animating my body, or the bodies of my friends. How otherwise could I account for the strange emotions I experienced? "Glimpses of glory ne'er forgot," of which the poet Wordsworth sings, which came like the remembrances of long-forgotten scenes! Wordsworth, orthodox thinker that he was, realised the truth of this gift of the soul.

Poets and romancers are said to entertain many vagaries, and this was one of mine. In some of my novels I have endeavoured to demonstrate this my belief.

Since I have become a denizen of the Spirit-world, I have found the doctrine of Pre-existence to be a truth, but not true in the sense in which I then understood it.

Pre-visions to which I and my brother authors are sometimes subject (among those favoured in this manner, I will mention Byron, Shelley, Dickens, Coleridge, and Wordsworth), are the result of the soul's actual experience. The spirit of every man of genius is capable of taking long flights away from the body in moments of abstraction, or in dreams. I say the soul of the man of genius, because the soul of the unemotional man is incapable of leaving the body for any length of time, or for any distance. I now fully believe that I had traversed, in spirit, this beautiful portion of Italy of which I speak.

The past lies buried beneath the present. We unearth

a modern city, and we find buried beneath it the temples and towers of a forgotten capital; so with many of our illustrious men of to-day, someone of the ancient heroes or poets, over whose ashes centuries have rolled, animate their frames and fire their veins. Not symbolically, but truly. The features, the hair, the eyes,—all represent the past hero. It may be Nero or Cæsar, Homer or Dante. They each betray through their new representatives unmistakable marks of their origin.

Men of the present experience many of the sensations of those of the past. When I walked with intoxicated ardour through the groves of cyprus and orange on the lakes of Como and Maggiore, I experienced the same sensations that poets of past ages have realised before me; and in this sense, as thoughts and feelings of kindred spirits mingle, is the doctrine of Metempsychosis realised.

Another mystery I have learned since I have entered Hades: it is that spirits of antiquity often select a promising child who may be born upon earth, for the purpose of directing its destiny, and controlling it for a special end.

Many times their projects are frustrated by opposing forces. Some individuals on earth whom I have seen, have as numerous a train of spirits attending them, as a king has courtiers. In many cases, these are in harmony; in others, they oppose each other's objects and aims.

The belief that was held by many ancient philosophers, that the souls of men enter into the bodies of animals, is true in a mystical sense. A spirit is incapable of acting, except through matter, and in those countries where the belief is prevalent, through the psychological influence of this belief the spirit really does control the animal, and an animal that is held in sacred reverence is taken possession of by certain spirits.

The human form is certainly the highest type of matter, through which the soul can manifest, but the lower orders of animals possess brains, and sensations, and *physiques* analogous to man's. These can certainly be controlled by spirits, but spirits generally seek the highest type of perfection by which they can communicate.

It is not my wish ever to animate a dog, a cow, or even a bird; but if I were communicating with a people who believed that the highest spiritual manifestations could come through a bull that they possessed, I should not hesitate to control that animal.

Through the dim vistas of centuries the traditions of the past are handed down,—through the long ages belief in the transmigration of souls appears at distant periods, the long-forgotten customs of the past are revived in the present; the urns that held the ashes of the dead, centuries ago, are being moulded again in the nineteenth century.

The transmigration of souls is a great truth and great mystery. I hope to exist centuries to come, and to animate some kindred soul in some newer and more distant sphere of existence.

ART NOTES.

TITIAN.

THE approach of Titian was marked by a spirit of exaltation, combined with a quiet dignity that was truly impressive. His utterances, like his works, were imbued with a feeling of refinement and selectness, and seemed to be the outflowing of a deep, penetrative nature.

In giving this slight sketch he would appear at times to be lifted up, as it were, into an ecstatic condition; or it might be that he had descended from that high state, and was still wrapt in an aura of transcendent feeling. Pacing the floor and gesticulating with Italian grace, the medium seemed an embodiment of noble grandeur.

December 9th, 1876.

AMATISSIMA AMICA,

OU call me from my home above the clouds, from the land of love. I have loved you for many years. When you have studied my designs I have been by your side; when you and your *sposa* visited my home in Venice I was with you.

Venice, the Queen of the Sea, rising like a spirit on the bosom of the Adriatic,—Venice, my home for almost a hundred years, I love thee still!

I sat by your side in the gondola, I walked with you on the piazza, I followed you through the narrow streets till you reached the very ground where my house, with its garden, once stood; there I painted during so many happy years, and I still paint in my spirit-home—in my home among the stars, where I have a studio. There I have my pictures of the most beautiful and divine ladies, which I would love to show you, so lovely are the women of this land, which is the home of love and beauty.

It fills me with the passions of gratification and remorse when I see so many who would study my colour, imitate it like a cloak, a mantle, from the outside, but who will not penetrate into the interior, will not infuse the love, the warmth, the soul of divine nature into their works.

From the sea, from the mountain, from beauty I realised my inspiration. Therein lies the secret of what my friends so kindly call my splendid colour.

If I could impart my manner I would do so, if it would be of use to mankind; but each man should work out his own style, should elaborate his own ideas.

When I trod upon earth, the painters of my day had a peculiar manner of preparing their canvas. They painted the ground red, because in analysing nature they found beneath the skin a red colour.

Over this ground, at times, they placed a thin skin of a lighter shade, resembling the natural skin, and upon this put in their figures. When the design was finished—a Venus, a Flora, or a Bella—we washed it over with an amber glaze, or a preparation of glue and wax, to prevent it from cracking, and, when dry, but before it hardened, we would spat it with a broom of fine threads, which lightly broke up the surface. As the most beautiful colours were discovered under the rays of the declining sun, or the soft rays of early morning, we selected those hours of the day when colour appeared the most mellow.

In my native land the sun shone with a subdued warmth,

never displaying the northern sharp, cutting lights; and we loved not the garish sunshine, neither did we love the shadow. The delicious light between the two is the light for colour; that is the light in which the orange fruit and the lemon appear the loveliest.

I lived nearly a century on this earth, and I have lived a few more centuries in Spirit-land, but I feel adolescent, I feel not aged. I love to visit this planet; I love to voyage with this medium, whom you sent to my native land, fair Italia. I have visited, with you both, Firenze. I have seen, through the eyes of this medium, my paintings in the Pitti Palace and in the Uffitzi Gallery, and it has given me pleasure, delight, to see again what had become obscure to me.

I perceive that the Venus in the Tribune has lost its life; that those who do not love me have washed away the last touches of my hand.

I have endeavoured to paint through mediums many times, but I am discouraged. My hand fails on earth; it follows not my mind entirely through the medium.

I am told that all mediums fail to be fully inspired in whatsoever way they are influenced. I say this that you may not expect too much. We give what we can, and you will receive what you can.

My heart is full of graciousness to-night that I have been able to speak, that this lovely lady has graciously submitted to my faulty influence.

I see a distant star dimly arising over the earth. Over three hundred years ago it rose in Venice, the land of colour. It shone over the Venetian School of Art.

Since then it has been lighting up distant planets, and may return again to this earth. I salute you with joy as harbingers of this rising star. Friends, *addio*.

MY PASSAGE TO SPIRIT-LIFE.

ABRAHAM LINCOLN.

THIS truly great patriot, accompanied by Secretary Seward and other members of State, visited our spirit-soirée and gave the following account of his "Passage to Spirit-Life." Mr. Lincoln held the important and conspicuous position of President of the United States during the memorable time when the country was embroiled in intestine war.

After grave deliberation he issued the "Emancipation Proclamation," which aroused the ire of the "Southern Rebels," as they were termed, and ultimated in his assassination while attending a representation in Ford's Theatre, Washington, in company with his wife and friends. The communication was given in a thoughtful, conversational style, occasionally breaking into the humorous, as was his manner on earth. At the point where he speaks of aiding the South, one of our company stated that 10 per cent. interest bonds had been purchased by a Northern man to assist the development of Alabama (a Southern State), after which she repudiated her obligations. Upon this Mr. Lincoln jocosely answered: "Then you are all rogues together,"—alluding to the Northerner taking 10 per cent. interest.

IT is scarcely necessary to allude to the manner of my death, as it is well known to the public. The feelings that attended my "taking off" affect me even now. There is something, to the spirit, truly awful in being called from the scene of active life without a moment's warning, without opportunity to bid adieu to friends, to embrace long-tried companions—with not one brief moment afforded, for settling affairs of life and transacting necessary business, before a final departure from the shores of Time. Mine was truly a sublime and awful exit! Not that I was entirely unprepared; I had long felt that a dark cloud overhung my sky, and had forbodings of some strange, undefined calamity awaiting me; I felt it when I entered that theatre at Washington. Some morbidly pious individuals, who undertake to think for the good Lord, have considered my assassination as a judgment upon me for visiting a play-house, but they will discover when they reach *this Port*, as a good clergyman remarked concerning the great disaster at the Brooklyn Theatre, that it matters not if a man leave for his Eternal Home from a theatre or from a church, providing he is prepared for the journey. *I was* prepared, inasmuch as I believed that every public officer should hold his life in his hand, ready to lay it down in the nation's service; and from the moment that it was revealed to me that I was chosen to release the slave from bondage, from that moment I felt that I was foredoomed, and I was willing that my life should be sacrificed for that necessary accomplishment.

On that fatal night which ended with my life's tragedy, when I fell mortally wounded in the theatre, and after a few moments of anguish—a brief time of mental despair, followed by unconsciousness—I awakened to find myself a spirit among spirits, and to realise that I was being actually crowned with a wreath of laurels by the hand of Washington, and that I was surrounded by an innumerable company of spirits "which no man could number,"—when I heard the grand vibrations of heavenly music surging through the air, filling my soul with an ecstatic bliss beyond mortal comprehension; then a weight was removed from my heart, and

I experienced a happiness that I had not felt for *ten long years!*

Spirits of the Next World are intimately connected with mortals, how intimately I never realised until I became a denizen of the Summer-land. Then I found that the inhabitants of that shadowy realm were perfectly familiar with my life, and under the direction of a wise power they had raised me from obscurity, and had elected me to be the Liberator of the Southern slaves. They had foreseen the dangers that encompassed me, and had used every effort to notify me of the plot in preparation to take my life. They had warned me again and again through mediums and my own clairvoyance. They knew the danger, but failed to avert it!

Thy foresaw also the long train of evils that would follow the emancipation of the negroes—blighting the fair South, and producing temporary destruction to bring about a future state of progress.

But such is the order of life! The field must be mowed down before it can grow another and better kind of grain. A plantation looks bare and unsightly, when the white cotton is stripped from the pod, and sent off to the looms; but it returns again in the form of a beautiful fabric which will clothe multitudes. So I believe it will be with the South.

She is like the stripped plantation now, but she will receive benefits untold, in the form of renewed energy, and freedom from debasing tyranny.

It shall be no longer *North* and *South*, but one people. The Northerners must help the Southerners build their factories, lay their railroads, and strive in every way to aid them in reconstructing their fallen fortunes.

I wish to say a few words about my wife; it has given me

great grief to see her treated as an insane person. Some thought I was not altogether right, because I had peculiar dreams and visions, and sometimes consulted mediums; but I must inform them that those who scoff at these things are more insane than they who believe in them.

It is said, that Spiritualism fills the insane asylums. If any cause could render a woman insane, the distressing events which attended and followed my sudden departure were sufficient to have made my wife so. But her belief in spirit-communion upheld and sustained her, and it was only through a misunderstanding of spirit-direction that she placed herself in a situation whereby she could have such a charge brought against her; but we hastened to her rescue and inspired some receptive noble minds to secure her release from a living tomb.

I do not know that it is necessary for me to speak about the present difficulties of the country, or to applaud General Grant's course, though I heartily do.*

It is impossible to put this country back on its onward march of progress, but bad men will arise now and then and hold office. It is not always possible to judge between a demagogue and a true lover of his country. One who makes the loudest assertions, swears the strongest, and promises the greatest—that one will naturally attract the ignorant. Boys will always turn from the rising sun to look at a bonfire. I remarked while I was in the White House, how much more show was made by the liveried servant than by his master.

Grant, who seems so quiet and befogged behind the smoke of his cigar, is a perfect master of the situation. Do not force him to don the livery and make a harlequin of

---

* Delivered while General Grant was filling his last term of office, the winter of 1876-77, Dec. 16.

himself, as he would do if he followed the advice of the thousands who beset him.

A soldier is better with two legs, but if one has been cut off, he had better wear a wooden leg than none at all. The nation has lost one of its legs, the South is trying to take away its wooden one (that is the *black votes*) and make it run on one. I tell you it will not run long.

DEATH BY FIRE.

CHARLOTTE CUSHMAN.

The following communication by the distinguished American *tragédienne*, was given just after the disastrous conflagration of the Brooklyn Theatre, by which a large number of individuals were burned to death, and the city was shrouded in mourning at the sad event. The whole population were deeply imbued with sorrow, and the very air was filled with thoughts connected with the accident.

The sympathies of the actress flowed toward those thus bereaved, and she expressed her feelings with a sincerity which showed that though absent in form she was present in spirit, desiring to aid from her enlightened standpoint the sorrowing ones of earth.

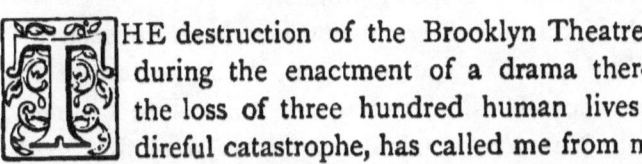HE destruction of the Brooklyn Theatre by fire during the enactment of a drama therein, and the loss of three hundred human lives by that direful catastrophe, has called me from my retirement. While this sad event has awakened a sensation of deepest sympathy amongst all classes, in the Spirit-world, it has especially excited those of the dramatic profession.

A tragedy more sublime has been enacted on that Brooklyn stage than could be ever depicted by the greatest master of the histrionic art! Mankind stands aghast, appalled at the fearful result.

To the eye of sense, death by fire seems terrific, yet aside from the terror produced, the sensation of passing away to spirit-life through fiery flames is not so painful as it is usually supposed to be. The soul and flame are congenial elements.

Man's nature is always attracted by a conflagration: something within him responds to the fire. The higher it kindles, the more enthusiastic he becomes: his soul rises with the ascending flames !

Eastern nations in all times have worshipped fire as the great purifying element. For them it is the source of life, and in this case it has proved to be the source of spiritual life to hundreds ! And though we deplore the accident on account of the misery to friends it brings with it, and the distress occasioned by such sudden and painful separation, yet seen from a spiritual point of view, it is not so fearful a disaster.

If it were not for man's genius, and did he not possess his wonderful powers of invention, he would be the most helpless of creation: at the mercy of wind, wave, and fire ; but most of the marvellous appliances of civilisation have grown out of calamities such as this one.

You ask if this event could not have been foreseen and prevented by spirits ? I answer, that, in the portion of the Spirit-land where I reside, and which is in close magnetic relation with New York and Brooklyn, we were first made acquainted with the danger portending, by the ringing of our peculiar alarm bells, which are stationed at various points for the purpose of indicating any extraordinary event that may occur in either city.

The spirit-guides and immediate relatives of those in the building saw the approaching peril before the audience were aware of it, and endeavoured to forewarn the assembly, but it is almost impossible to make persons unfamiliar with spirit-communion aware of the information or impression their spirit-friends may try to give them.

Mr. and Mrs. Conway were especially interested in the theatre, which has borne their name, and their spirits hastened immediately to the scene of disaster, and were there in time to warn many of the performers, and impress the most susceptible ones to hasten to places of safety.

Mr. Murdock, one of the young and talented actors, who lost his earth-life, tells me that he became paralysed immediately his spirit-friends began to admonish him of his imminent peril. The effect was to throw him into a sort of stupor or trance, in which he only realised a great light around him like the rising sun. When he became conscious, and found himself in the arms of dear friends who had passed away from earth, he thought for a moment he had escaped from the burning theatre, not realising that he had entered into spirit-life !

One of the greatest sights I have ever witnessed was that of last night, when the crowd of helpless spirits took shape in spirit-form above the burning theatre! Most of the working-men and mechanics were anxious to return home, and could not realise their change of condition, or the spirit-life they had entered upon.

This host of people we were obliged to provide immediately with garments, and for this purpose we had all supplied ourselves with white cloaks, such as are uniformly used for wrapping around the newly-born spirit-form; they are of a light gossamer material, and very beautiful to the eye, of a texture resembling silk and silver, something between the two.

Man is as helpless as regards his clothing when born into the Spirit-world as when he enters the material sphere. After the excited parties were clothed they were permitted to depart to their earth-homes, accompanied by spirit-guides, where they will probably remain for a few days, seeking vainly to converse with their friends: after which I suppose they will be more satisfied to make their pilgrimage to the Land of Spirits. I speak thus, for so it was in my case.

I have been a mere idler since I came here,—that is, so far as I have been engaged in any visible occupation; but I have been deeply occupied in studying the habits and customs of this country, and every day I find more and more to interest me, and to "awaken my especial wonder."

I am surprised at the systematic, wise, and benevolent plans that have been adopted for receiving new comers from earth. This large body of prematurely-born people will be amply provided for; their friends need have no fears. They will not certainly be placed in palaces, nor forced to live lives of blissful ease, but will be assigned places in accordance with their development, and will commence life again as young persons just budding into manhood.

Theatres are supposed by many to be a source of evil, and this sad destruction will be looked upon by such persons as an evidence of God's displeasure. But the great God who made the earth, and created man with all his faculties and desires, only seeks man's development and progress; whatsoever will further that end He will sanction. That is my humble opinion, from what I have seen of this superior world.

The personation of character and the delineation of passions are products of one of man's spiritual faculties. In the early ages, before the art of printing was understood, the great multitude were only taught of the world around them through these means, and they thus became acquainted with events of great moment and historical interest. Dramatic representations were man's earliest means of conveying intelligence to the multitude.

The burning of this theatre should be a lesson to teach men to provide exits of safety for the public, and should cause advances to be made in the construction of your public buildings.

If but one or two great amphitheatres were constructed in a city as places of public amusements, as in olden times, and the expense concentrated on one or two edifices; and if they were built so strongly that they would defy earthquakes and fire, like the amphitheatres of Rome and Pompeii, we would not be obliged to chronicle an event such as this.

December 7, 1876.

THE PRESENT STATE OF THE DRAMA.

EDWIN FORREST.

THE eminent American tragedian, Edwin Forrest, was requested to contribute a few thoughts relating to his profession and experience in spirit-life, and in an agreeable manner he responded to our wishes.

He first desired one of the company to read a passage from Shakespeare, the author to whom his life-study had been devoted.

In accordance with his wish, an act from "King Lear" was recited, which interested him much, while the grand and touching sentiments of the immortal bard seemed to stir his dramatic love, and also to revive sad memories of the capriciousness of popular applause, and the insecurity of an actor's position when he becomes an idol of the public.

Still he was thoughtful and philosophic, and with some interest recalled a project of establishing a Dramatic College, which the writer had proposed to him some years previously.

THAT scene from "King Lear" stirs my soul within me, and reminds me of my last days on earth. Alas! I, too, was then a poor king, stripped of his crown. My kingdom had passed from me. I walked the stage like that poor dethroned monarch, and wore a crown of faded flowers, the semblance of the former one which I had worn.

It is a sad event for a man whose dramatic career has been crowned with honours, who has heard the deafening applause of multitudes, who has been followed and fêted year after year, until he really feels himself to be a king, to find himself, like Lear, despoiled of his followers, and the clamour and hurrah that attended his early appearance hushed down to the timid cheer of a few faithful friends.

Truly, such a winding up of a famous career is enough to cause an actor to make a hasty exit from the scene of his former triumphs!

Public taste changed very much in the interval between my entrance upon the dramatic stage and my leaving it.

The public no longer seemed to comprehend the merit of true dramatic art. I say this, not as especially applying to myself, though I must acknowledge that it chafed and grieved me to witness the demand for mere imitation, and literal rendering of passions and sentiments.

My idea of histrionic art is, that it should represent the broad general aspect of nature, and that if a murder is to be enacted, it should not be a narrow, cold-blooded performance of the deed, but a heroic action, such as Shakespeare described it to be, and as all inspired actors render it.

The present demand for sensational plays and domestic dramas, which do not elevate the taste or sentiment of the people, is, I am happy to think, destined to be short-lived, it being merely a temporary fashion. The instinct of the people will draw them back to true and solid ground. While there are such immortal examples in the past to look to, people cannot go very far astray.

You ask, do I tread the boards in the Spirit-world, or Summer-land, as it is called.

I have given a few representations, but very few as yet— I find so much to interest me off the stage. My nature is more thoroughly satisfied here than it was on earth. I have much to learn, and spend a portion of my time in travelling. I am happy to see, that, the "Home for Actors," which it was my good fortune to be able to leave on earth, is opened. I visit there occasionally, but I cannot say that I am much attracted to earth. I have had enough of it, its good, and its bad, and perhaps my organisation was such, that I attracted more of its bad than of its good. Be that as it may, I am more contented where I am.

When I play here, there are no empty boxes. The weak shams that are so popular on earth, cannot find foothold in this realm. Yet I do not wish to be severe; it is my nature to speak strongly, but it is a misforture for a people to live on the external, and to neglect the ideal.

CHRISTMAS CAROLS.

CHARLES DICKENS.

It was a cold, dark evening in December; the snow fell heavily in the streets of New York; we had not thought of Dickens, and knew not what was coming, when the medium closed her eyes and began, as though declaiming from a book, the following carols.

She relates that she seemed to see before her the scene as Dickens depicts it; she was apparently out upon the roadside, saw the distant cathedral, and beheld the poor old man lying there, as though it were a real event or a scene in a theatre.

CAROL No. I.

NOW, as the dark days approach, nearing the holidays, I feel again like using my pen.

Do you ever ask yourselves, friends, what sort of a Christmas we have up here? Do you ever inquire whether there is any gathering around the fire, by those whom you love, in the Spirit-world?

There was one sort of fire we were taught to dread when we were young. It was said to burn with everlasting malignity, and the poor wight who had gone astray on earth was sure to be bundled into it, on emerging from Time into Eternity! *That's* the sort of fire for Christmas holidays among good Christians.

I recall the poetry of a dark day by the Christmas fire, for the memory of those holidays on earth is too fresh to have faded from my mind. The Christmas we celebrate here is but the shadow of our past earthly festivities; for, are we not living in an eternal Christmas?

We hear the echo of your Christmas chimes resounding in our spirit-homes, though in truth from many a spirit-spire our own chimes peal out gladly, blending with yours in joyous harmony.

Listen! ye rapt souls! Do ye not hear our heavenly bells chiming on your Christmas mornings? Ring out, glad bells, and welcome poor shivering souls into this happy land! Ring out, Spirit-world Christmas bells, for the poor who die on Christmas Days! Poor homeless waifs of humanity, for once they shall have a merry Christmas!

I have passed many a Christmas on earth in dear old England, the remembrance of which causes me a thrill of happiness, but in the Spirit-world only a few have I seen; and for this reason I cannot speak as wisely as I otherwise might of the varied modes of celebrating the day in these eternal cities; but my experience is, that Christmas is celebrated here, and the carol of "Peace on earth, and good-will to man," is commemorated in the everlasting world, with even greater joy than it is on earth.

"Peace on earth, and good-will to man," is the chant which I am told was actually sung by a vast company of spirits, who convened for that purpose eighteen hundred years ago; and every returning year, that same carol is echoed by innumerable bands of immortals.

On two occasions I have joined these celebrants. I was told how, in the far past, good spirits were moved to distress and pity, to know that the prevailing belief among mankind was, that the Rulers of the Spirit-world were at enmity with man! How sadly it grieved them to know that every tempest, and every plague was attributed to their influence!

When that bright particular *Star* was born in Bethlehem, who was to lead man into a higher perception of his spiritual nature, rapturously they sang that famed Christmas chant, which will stand so long as the world stands, and will be repeated in the Spirit-world, and on earth through centuries of time to come!

CAROL No. 2.

Down, down falls the Christmas snow! circling down in soft baby-like flakes, as white-souled messengers from an

[illegible due to damage] ... sore and hungry, crouching ... He tossed up his last copper on Christmas Eve, and lost that; he has had a long, long tramp since, and has been groping over those cold, long, weary miles, for some stray coin dropped by his god, *Chance*,—the only God he has ever known!

Chance has frowned on him this Christmas Day, and he sinks exhausted by the way-side. Poor old Buffer! Friendless, and homeless, wifeless and childless; it has gone hard with him this merry Christmas, and he thinks as he sits there, too nerveless to rise, what a lucky chance it would be if some fine gentleman should pass by and drop him a sixpence or a shilling for his Christmas.

Faintly sound upon his ear the happy chimes from the distant cathedral tower. Soft and white the snow falls, creeping nearer and nearer, like some sheltering friend; and his hungry, eager gaze dies out in a helpless look of endurance.

The snow falls faster and faster; the cold pierces deeper and deeper; he makes an effort to rise, but he cannot; his limbs are stiff with cold and famine, and yet life is dear to him. Life has been with him a constant conflict with the elements, a mere animal struggle for existence, against earth's contending forces; and now, in his last moments, his only thought and wish is, that some kind gentleman would give him a sixpence, wherewith to buy a mug of ale and a slice of bacon for his Christmas dinner.

Ring out, Christmas bells! another immortal soul is about to commence a long tramp over the Unknown Highway!

The snow falls white; his weary body and tattered garments are alike covered by its pure cold robe. Now slowly he raises his half-palsied arm and touches his battered cap. He is making his exit from the world! He bows, but it is to a phantom gentleman, who suddenly stands before him. He is too far gone to question whence he came. Is it the kind gentleman with the friendly sixpence, whom he has been looking for? Is he some good Christian from the cathedral town who has heard his hungry cry? or some noble lord from the neighbouring park? He dreamily asks himself these questions as the friendly person approaches nearer, takes him by the arm, and places to his parched lips a generous, life-reviving cordial.

Surely this must be the *chance* gentleman he has been all this Christmas Day thinking of. Presently this unknown friend lifts him from the snow-bound hedge, and leads him to a curious chariot, gay as the fiery chariot of Elijah. He resists at first; the kindness is too much for him; he is not used to such attentions, and shakes his head, and draws back. But when the gentleman, in answer to his hesitation, says, "Come, my friend, I will take you to a good inn, where you shall have your Christmas dinner," he yields to the good chance, and they vanish together.

Together they glide on, on, over the spires of the cathedral; they hear the chimes ring out for Christmas, but no one sees them in their golden chariot. The good Christians eat their dinner, and cast not one thought to the poor wretches dying from cold and hunger, beneath the snowy hedges of merry old England, on Christmas Day!

Ring out, Spirit-world Christmas bells, for the poor who die on Christmas Days! Poor homeless waifs of humanity, for once they shall have a merry Christmas!

AN
OPIUM-EATER's DREAM OF HEAVEN.

DE QUINCEY.

IT is the desire of Judge Edmonds and Countess Ossoli, the spirit-editors of this work, to show that in migrating to another world, persons retain their identity and peculiar habits of thought, and they urge upon each author to display, as far as possible, his natural characteristics through the clairvoyante. The following sketch by De Quincey, is considered to bear the marks of its talented author. The medium, under his control, experienced a blissful, ecstatic condition, and, though never having seen the Nile, realised in her trance, that she was floating down that sacred river; anon the scene changed, and she felt as though in the utmost bounds of space, probably partaking of feelings similar to those experienced by the spirit.

AVE you ever been an opium-eater? Have you ever had an afflatus upon you so deliriously stimulating, that the whole universe seemed to you like an exquisite diapason of soft music and colour?

Dreamily, dreamily I have floated down the Egyptian Nile, and watched the sun setting with yellow splendour beyond its strange waters. I have stood upon the top of the highest pyramid—sat down before the great Sphinx and looked into its mysterious eyes—seen the moon rise in weird glory over the temple of Thebes—have felt the kiss of the most beautiful of women trembling upon my lips—have had visions of fairy loveliness,—but these experiences all pale and become as mist before the transcendent realities which open to a spirit's sight!

Imagine yourself capable of flying to the top of the highest mountain on earth, and beyond this, suppose yourself in space, the air scintillating with light, and that through this illimitable space you are wheeling; around you speed gorgeous balls of light, glowing with varied colours of amethyst ruby, topaz, and emerald dyes, like mammoth gems whirling through the air, while beyond this pyrotechnic revolution of worlds, you behold afar off the Land of Souls!

Among these scenes of sublimity you pursue your solitary way till you reach the confines of a new world; not diminutive, like the earth you have left, but a sphere whose vast dimensions are as the sun in size, and which, like that orb, seems to be a globe of light.

A strange tremor pervades your frame, an ardent desire, a longing possesses you to attain to this world and penetrate its atmosphere, which envelops it like a phosphorescent halo. You obey this instinct, and as the bird aloft in the heavens dives through the air for its food, so the soul with unerring instinct descends through this luminous atmosphere and finds its food—its kindred also! Kindred! thousands and thousands of years old! Here are those first sons of earth who lived in the Garden of Eden! here is the great Hebrew leader MOSES, six thousand years old; here are the mighty captains, those fiery leaders of the hosts who fought in battle for Liberty and God, in the earlier ages of the world. Here are the great personages of history: King Cyrus is here; Alexander the Great is here; here is Zenobia, the famed captive Queen; here are Cæsar Augustus, Marc Anthony, Cleopatra with her lovers; here are

Demosthenes and Cicero, Dante and Petrarch; here are Raphael and Michael Angelo,—all passed out of the earth's dominions, phantoms on the page of history: here they are, living in this World of Spirits!

Is it not a magnificent opium dream? Are these fair cities real? Are these trees and shrubs, these mountains and plains, substantial and real, or is it all the dream of an opium-eater? Is this a real world—this electric ball which flashes like a jewel, and whirls through space like the chariot-wheels of Jehovah?

Is it true that these powerful beings, with their many faculties, once inhabited that tiny globe called Earth? These wonderful beings who can traverse the air like arch-angels, who whirl through space like flaming meteors, were they once toilers over the heavy sands of earth?

Look out upon the heavens and count the stars! More numerous than those shining points are the homes of souls in eternity!

Where there is no beginning, there is no end; and from where I stand upon the opal heights, I can see in creation neither beginning nor end!

Is this the dream of an opium-eater? It is what I see; it is what all spirits see. What wonder that we are powerless to express visions thus unfolded to our view! Who can describe men who have lived twenty thousand years? What mortal tongue can express the wonders that pass before eyes which have been looking on spirit-life thousands of centuries! If men fail to understand the workings of the little globe Earth, how can they comprehend the plans of this mighty World of Souls?

My opium dream is o'er. I no longer need the stimulus of that fatal drug to awaken my faculties. I breathe an air so refined that it permeates my being, and lifts me up among the gods! I am no longer a mortal, weak and ailing, shrinking from the storms of earth, but an immortal, ever-progressing inhabitant of a world whose breath is like the finest air of summer as it steals over a garden of perfumed flowers.

SPIRIT-FLOWERS.

FANNY FERN.

IT was a disagreeable Sunday evening in New York. The medium had been in the house all day, and felt weary and rather averse to being influenced. However, she consented to be put in the mesmeric sleep, hoping it would restore her nervous power. Immediately, the spirit of Fanny Fern took possession of her, and presented her with the spirit-flowers she had gathered. The medium saw them in all their beauty, and returned to her natural state smiling and light-hearted.

HAVE been out all day in the fields, gathering flowers. See what a beautiful bouquet I have collected! Here are violets more fragrant than the famed violets of Parma; lilies and roses too, the dear old favourites of earth; and besides I have brought delicious rose-coloured bells, with creamy stamens and petals, sending forth an odour like pine apples; and rare feathery flowers growing on a large stem,—fit home for some fairy spirit!

The Spirit-world must certainly have been the cradle of flowers! for here they bloom in a profusion only shadowed forth in your own tropical clime. Flowers truly are an expression of the soul; they belong to the spirit. People on earth recognise this truth when they are in exalted moods.

They cover their dead with them; they are the only offering brought to the passing soul!

Most of the higher expressions of the heart are denoted by flowers. You decorate the bride with orange-blossoms, and place her fair head beneath a floral bell! The lover gives them to the queen of his heart, and spirits place them before their mediums. Every clairvoyant describes beautiful flowers with which the spirits are crowned, and groups of angelic children are seen dispensing these fragrant offerings. I have noticed that people smile incredulously when told of the realities of the Spirit-world, but they never disbelieve that flowers grow there! The most sceptical receive this statement as a natural one, forgetting, that if our soil be adapted to the growth of flowers, it must also be adapted to trees and other kind of vegetation.

I have even found here the dear old fern of earth—my namesake! of which I have seen most beautiful varieties, delicate lacy patterns which seem like the breath of God petrified. Beside flowers, I have with me bunches of strawberries—delicious, pyramidal berries, just as palatable to spirit-taste as they were to me in earth days.

I live here a free life; no more care; the laws that bind me are like a chain of flowers: I feel not their weight. No more does the fear of not pleasing assail me. Like a bird I go and come, when I will and where I will. I visit, I enter my neighbour's dwelling without knocking. The houses of earth are to me like glass, or straw more like; I see through the cracks and crevices clearly.

I now discover that evil is only the result of circumstances. The flower that is kept in the cellar cannot bloom; and he who would develop his highest nature must be like the flowers, and let the sunlight, the air, and the winds of heaven reach him from all quarters. He must not shut off any truth, nor stint his nature in any healthful direction—then will he be able to enjoy this gracious spirit-life.

Oh, how I should like to take with me on this Sabbath day, some stiff, austere, old, puritanic brother through my garden of flowers! How shocked will the narrow religionist feel when he enters this World of Flowers. Will he hunt for strawberries, think you, on the Sabbath day as I do, and thankfully enjoy nature as God made it? or will he refuse, and turn from the spirit-flowers and ripe fruit, vainly seeking rest as now, outside of God and nature?

I must hasten back to my tent of fern leaves, whither, when you come to this flowery land. dear reader, I will lead you.

THE STORY OF THE GREAT KING.

HANS CHRISTIAN ANDERSEN.

No doubt any person familiar with the noted story-teller would have recognised his presence by his manner, through the medium, as he related his own spirit-experience under the guise of a tale; for the "Visit to the Great King" is really, he says, a transcript of what occurred to him on his arrival in the Next World.

OW, I will tell you a little story. Once upon a time there was a poor young man living in a distant city. His father was poor and his mother was poor, but they were industrious; and though they lived in a little room in a large city, they loved Nature; and of the crumbs from their frugal repast the son scraped and fed the little birds that came to their window and lived upon their housetop. Any green plant or shrub he could get he would foster, and it would grow beneath his loving care, for his heart was in sympathy with Nature.

Well, this young man, sitting alone at his work, would see the most beautiful visions, which would fill his soul with gladness; so he could not but speak of what he saw. The neighbours, learning this, would gather around him to hear him talk, and describe the lovely though invisible scenes

In the course of time, boys and girls from far and near would come to hear his talk, and the rich ones brought him presents, so that he need no longer work at his lowly trade, but could spend all his time in describing his wonderful visions.

And as wealth came to him, he grew stronger, and his voice became more powerful, and after a time he left his humble home and set out to visit strange cities.

Wherever he went he told his wondrous tales, and the people flocked about him, and took him to their homes, and loaded him with presents, and he grew daily more and more prosperous. But all this time he had not forgotten his sweet teacher, *Nature*, nor the Great Father who had given him eyes to see the glorious sun, and the moon, and trees, and flowers, and the fruitful earth; and a heart to feel, to love and to sympathise with the troubled, the heart-broken, and the unfortunate!

He had many friends. Kings and queens invited him to sit at their table, and he ate and drank with nobles. But of all the people around him he loved best little children, because they were simple and truthful, and they returned his love; they followed him wherever he went, so that he was never alone.

But as days and years passed, while he sang, and told his strange stories, he began to grow old and his voice to fail him.

Then word came from the King of a distant land, that he must forsake all of his friends, lay aside his wealth, and honours, and go and dwell with him.

Now, this King was represented to him as a dreadful being who had two places to which he consigned all those unwary travellers who ventured to visit him. One place was a dreadful lake of flaming liquid pitch, into which he delighted to thrust those who displeased him; and the other was a place where they all sat and sang triumphal hymns over those poor tortured beings.

In such dread was this King held by the people of the surrounding countries, that they put on long robes of black, and covered their faces with heavy veils, and hung from their hats long streamers of black crape, to denote the sorrow and woe they experienced when the summons came from this inexorable King for their friends to visit his dreaded and unknown Kingdom.

This poor man, to whom the earth was so lovely and whose friends were so kind, and who had beguiled so many with his stories, could not beguile this mighty King. He had to comply with his orders, and go empty-handed into the strange country.

He had to lay aside in the drawers the fine suits of clothes he had acquired. He looked with longing eyes at the books of his library, wishing he could pack them in his trunk, and take them with him; but the messengers denied his request, for no one is permitted to take anything with him to that great King's kingdom!

All that he had accumulated in his years of toil—his birds and his flowers, his money in the bank, his possessions which he had gained by care and industry, he was forced to leave.

So he took a sad farewell from his friends, and looked his last upon the cheerful sun, and started forth on his lonesome voyage.

It was dark at first, the air was thick with gloomy mist, and the wind blew, but he said to himself, "I will keep up my courage, for it cannot be but that the All-Wise One who superintends the heavens and the earth, and who protects the little flowerets so that they grow up sheltered amid the storms of winter by the side of the rocks—it cannot be but that He will protect me."

Thus encouraging himself, he pursued his solitary way, which he thought would be exceedingly long. While thinking thus, he suddenly saw before him, not far distant, a city glowing in a light like that of the setting sun. As he gazed upon it he realised it to be the city of the fierce King; when suddenly there emerged from the avenue of trees that fringed its borders, a gay party of little children, who were dressed in all the charming colours of the blossoms that grow in the fields, and carried with them, in their hands and crowning their heads, the most wonderful flowers that were ever seen !

Smilingly they approached him, and some of the tallest among them stepped from among the others, and running to him lifted up their rosy lips to him and kissed the way-worn traveller, saying to him : "Thou art Hans Christian Andersen. We know thee ! Come, see what a beautiful garden we have made for thee."

And as they ceased speaking, the others circled around him, and, having grasped his hands and kissed his lips, led him away to the entrance of the shining city.

Lo ! there stood a garden, surrounded by hedges of what appeared to be roses, which were in full bloom, and filled the air with their fragrance, and as he stopped to admire the flowers, the children cried, " Come, come, dear friend, and see what else we have for thee ;" and they led him within to a lovely cream-coloured house, with a verandah on all sides, and vines clustering and creeping up to the very windows ! Just such a house as he had seen in his visions long days ago !

When he told them this, they clapped their hands with expressions of pleasure, and then led him within to an apartment where were arranged tastefully on shelves familiar books, that almost seemed to be the identical books he had left behind him so sorrowfully, when he set out to visit the wonderful King.

From this, the Room of Books, they led him to a friendly little *salon* on the opposite side, called the Room of Friendship, where, upon a round table, were placed the most beautiful dishes imaginable, cups and saucers, and plates so delicately tinted and painted, they looked like the petals of some flowers.

Still they proceeded on to a much larger room. This was called the Room of Song. There he beheld his favourite instruments of music—his flute, violin, and piano; and as he was looking with wonderment on them he heard a great sound without,—hundreds of voices rising in a song of welcome!

So exalted he became with joy and gratitude, that tears rained down from his eyes and blinded him, and the children gathered around him, brought him a chair covered with soft cushions, and seated him, so that he might listen and enjoy the music.

The song rose higher and higher, and as he listened he heard that it celebrated his arrival. Oh, what music was there! All the sweet sounds he had heard from his boyhood to his manhood were like gross mutterings compared with this ravishing melody.

When the song was complete the singers entered, and lo! among them were friends of his boyhood and of his manhood—dear people who had started long before him to obey the mandate of the stern King to visit his unknown Kingdom.

Oh, who can tell what greetings of joy arose when he met his long-lost friends and relatives! When their emotions could be controlled they sat down around him, and told him about the Great King,—how that he was a *Good King;* how he cared for everyone who visited his land; and that the dangerous lake was but a fable, like the fables of old; such as sailors in earlier days were wont to enliven their countrymen with.

They told him that the only lakes to be seen were the crystal streams, whose refreshing waters revivified the dwellers of that fairy-like land. They told him also that the Great King was invisible to them, but that they felt him in the balmy air, and that they recognised his presence in the song, and they felt his goodness by his ministering spirits—by the benevolence and goodness displayed around them in his kingdom, whereby a home was provided for the meanest voyager from earth to his country; for the humblest found a home and friends awaiting him.

And when they had finished their conversation, the beautiful children passed cups around to the vast company, filled with the most delicious beverage that lips ever tasted, and plates of fruit such as Eden never grew in her favoured soil,—for the richness, and flavour, and colour of the fruit of this marvellous Kingdom surpassed everything dreamed of.

And this ends my story of my journey to the Land of the Great King.

CHATEAU IN THE MIDST OF ROSES.

GEORGES SAND.

IF our readers could have heard the pretty broken French, and seen the truly foreign control of the medium, they would not have doubted the presence of the great novelist. She spoke of the distance she had come to visit America, and of her desire while on earth to see the New World, and how strange were her sensations in imparting her thoughts through a foreigner. The medium saw plainly her *chateau*, as she described it, and felt an exhilirating and joyous influence during Georges Sand's visit.

H, what a beautiful place is this heaven! I feel quite young again. I have seen myself reflected in a mirror, and I looked like a young girl of nineteen or twenty. I am no longer a grandmother, though I have my darlings around me. I have seen Auguste, Corneille, Le Blanc. I am so happy! Life means something for me now. People have called me *mauvaise*, because I was not a devotee, because I gave not much money to the priest, because I glorified human nature, because I celebrated the woman who had loved supremely; but I find that HERE I am not called a *bad woman!*

I find here for me a beautiful little *chateau* embowered in roses. Roses bloom in Spirit-land as well as on earth;

they are not alone for earth. My good friends come and
sit in my garden. I give them to eat of the delicious fruits
that grow here. Oh, what heroes have I had come to my
humble doors to welcome me! There were the Napoleons;
actually I saluted the Little Corporal! I spoke to him of
the past and the present of France—of my country ever
aspiring, ever arising, with hope after it has been crushed
to the dust! Napoleon is content while France is happy
and prosperous, but when he is needed he will re-appear.

Poets and musicians have called on me. Lamartine,
David, Auber, and *Rachel* no longer prostrate, but alive,
vivement! Rachel improvised for me a grand declamation
on my arrival. She represented the grief of the world at
parting with me, and the joy of my spirit-friends at my
coming among them. Oh, it is like Fairy-land here! I
was like Fanchon, a poor little beggar with scarcely any
attire. Now I am like Cinderella, after the godmother has
touched her with her wand!

I wish you could see my home. I have a charming
arbour where I write ; all has been so beautifully arranged
by my friends. It is decorated with the most lively
pictures, and embellished with flowers. I write at a table
inlaid with gems!—gems such as earth cannot offer, more
perfect in colour and transparency; so lucid and sparkling
that I should think you could almost see them shine on
your earth! This lovely home with its surroundings was
prepared for me by my friends.

In France we pay great court and respect to our friends
who have passed to another life, and always celebrate their
name day, and the anniversary of the day on which they
started on their immortal voyage; and in keeping them
thus in memory we unknowingly benefit ourselves; for I
find that those who remember their spirit-friends, and talk

with them confidingly, are better off here than those who coldly bury them, and give them up to Death.

The Roman Catholic religion is a grand religion for sentiment. I was a Liberalist, yet I did not believe exactly with Voltaire or Jean Jaques Rousseau. *Mon Dieu, je suis très content!* I have had an interview with Michelet. Ah, poor man, he has been so distracted! There is one misfortune in knowing all that transpires on earth—he realises *that*. I have known persons mesmerised on earth who could see what was transpiring at a distance, and it is in the same way that spirits can see what their friends are doing on earth. I can sit at my table and see what is being done on earth.

It is grand for me to convey my thoughts through this medium. This is my first voyage to America; it is pleasant to travel as the birds do! Latterly on earth I had not cared much for the travel, but now I find it agreeable to dart through space and go where I am attracted to. Now I will after this make many voyages.

It is quite a French society where I reside. I do not feel at home in your *Spring Garden*, in your America Spirit-world, though it is a beautiful country. But I will love all Americans, and like them to come and visit me. I find society here more like my dreams,—what you would call Utopian dreams! Utopian ideas are realised here.

How I have striven to make society more natural, to relieve it of its shams, to simplify the artificial structure, to equalise and classify people. The things that the French Socialists and Liberal writers have endeavoured to accomplish we find now already done in the Spirit-world for us: not as the Communists would effect it, ignorant and mistaken beings,—not by tearing down and despoiling, but by elevating and developing.

How people did cry against me at first because I thought

for myself, and not according to rules established in ignorance. I felt within my mind certain truths, and wished to express them. Blindly I groped my way—committed some errors against society, but felt that they were not against the God who created me, who was within me. Society sets up a standard for individuals, and punishes them if their conscience will not permit them to follow it. In this respect it needs remodelling.

My country has long been struggling for " Liberty, Equality, and Fraternity !" This is the motto of the inhabitants of the spheres.

Soon as I resume my pen I will write a romance of the Spirit-life. Dumas is travelling. I cannot speak of him, for he has gone to a distant world. He understood about this mystery better than I did. He was a medium, and was controlled by spirits, and comprehended spirit-communication. *Au revoir.*

THE SPIRIT - BRIDE.

MRS. GASKELL.

As the medium had often seen the spirit of Felicia Hemans dressed as a bride, with white veil and orange-blossoms, she desired to know why she assumed that garb. Mrs. Gaskell kindly offered to explain the mystery to the public as well as to the medium. The spirits of Josephine and Mary Queen of Scots, often appear thus attired.

URING my short residence in the Spirit-world I have had frequent opportunities for witnessing the power of spirit of attracting to itself whatever it may strongly desire to possess.

In one of the sunniest nooks to be found in the Summer-land is the poetic home of Felicia Hemans. Strange stories had reached my ear of the demands made upon her by mortals, and of the constant necessity she was subjected to of visiting earth to satisfy the longings of certain individuals who craved her presence. Accordingly I resolved to inquire into the matter, and to solve the mystery of the "Spirit-Bride," in which form I had been told the poetess often appeared.

Before my decease I had heard described in certain literary circles of England, the visits to earth, like meteors, of those veiled beings known as "Spirit-Brides;" and, anxious to obtain a solution of their enigmatical appearance, I sought an introduction to Felicia Hemans, which was readily obtained.

Upon reaching her residence (which resembled a Grecian temple embowered in trees), I found her under the portico, waiting to receive me, attired as a bride, in purest white, with a gauzy veil floating around her form, and a wreath of orange blossoms entwined in her hair, and her face beaming with happiness.

She placed me upon one of the light seats in the porch, remarking that she could remain with me but a short time then, as she had a call from earth, and must leave me for a few hours, after which she would return to me!

I begged her to permit me to accompany her, and, after reflecting a few seconds, she smilingly consented. We journeyed joyously together until we reached earth; there we entered a darkened room in some locality unknown to me, where a medium was holding a *seance*.

A gentleman of noble presence was peering in the darkness, and watching intently the folds of a curtain suspended over a corner of the apartment, to see it draw aside and disclose the form of his Spirit-Bride.

Mrs. Hemans, trembling and eager, advanced at his call. Rejoiced at the shadowy vision she presented, he demanded her to approach nearer. This she did. Apparently completely under his control, she performed obediently every wish he uttered. She kissed his forehead, placed a wreath of flowers upon his head, smoothed his hair, and floated back and forth before his gaze, that he might see the airy grace of her figure. Again and again he called for her, and she was detained in that darkened room for two hours, obedient and subservient to that man's will.

When we left, and had risen out of the stifling atmosphere,

I asked her why she went there. She replied that she could not resist, that he needed her, called her his "*bride,*" and that her presence elevated and benefited him, and go she *must.*

She further informed me that she found it impossible to resist any strong nature seeking her presence with high aspirations; that their desire strengthened and beautified her; that the gentleman I had seen felt her to be his bride, and accordingly she attired herself as a bride to gratify his eye and satisfy his taste. It was but a harmless diversion, as a mother would assume any particular dress to please her child, or a wife would adorn herself in any favourite attire to satisfy her husband; so she robed herself as a bride to please the idealities of those on earth who loved her, but that as many demands of the kind were made upon her, she performed her duties more like an actress, *con amore,* than like a veritable bride. "But I know," continued she, "of many young spirit-girls who have been betrothed to mortals and truly become the brides of their earthly spouse."

I felt that it would be impossible for a coarse, vulgar nature to attract such a spirit as Felicia Hemans; only those who resemble her in poetic sentiment and refined spiritual aspirations could magnetise and attract her noble, sympathetic spirit.

That the spirit possesses this wonderful power to attract its counterpart, is exemplified in the life of my gifted young friend Charlotte Bronté. When on earth she attracted the interest of a French Professor. Her fresh, earnest, pure nature, was to him a revealment such as he had never previously known.

She was a type of woman of which he had hitherto dreamed, but never seen. He became deeply interested in her, and psychologised by her spiritual temperament to that degree, that when she left his school and returned to her home on the Moors, he still retained a magnetic preception of her spiritual presence, and she likewise felt the thrill of his ardent masculine nature. An imperceptible magnetic thread extended between the two. His soul yearned for her constantly, and she felt it in her distant home across the Channel. When her sad and lonely pilgrimage on earth ended, and she entered her Summer-home, she still felt the cravings of her kind French master for her presence and strengthening influence.

She tells me that she, too, in her home among the immortals, felt for the lonely professor, and did all in her power to cheer and comfort him. Finally, when he gave up his hard and unsatisfying life and went to join her in Spirit-land, she rejoiced to regain once more his companionship.

There are many cases of obsession coming under my observation, where individuals have ceased to be themselves, so dominantly are they ruled by the spirit whom they have attracted. The doctrine of transmigration of souls is not a myth. Many persons on earth have pre-existed.

I know of a noble gentleman in England who, on seeing a spirit dressed in an oriental garb, recovered the memory of his past existence, and recalled the hours when he had wooed her hundreds of years ago on the shores of the Bosphorus.

LONE STAR:
AN INDIAN SPIRIT'S STORY.

FENNIMORE COOPER.

Persons familiar with Indian history, as connected with North America, will perceive in this narrative a deeper meaning than appears on the surface.

Mr. Cooper assures us that his tale is a true story, and that he received it direct from the lips of the Indian who is the hero of the little drama, and it proves that the red man has feelings and sensibilities quite as refined as the civilised white man. The destruction of the emigrants, known as the "Mountain Meadow massacre," actually occurred near Salt Lake, America. It was instigated by some deluded Mormons, as Mr. Cooper relates, who, disguised as savages, and aided by a small band of Indians, perpetrated the cruel massacre described in the tale. Recently (within three years), the Mormon leader who had escaped for fifteen or twenty years, was brought to justice, and executed for his action in this barbarous affair.

Fennimore Cooper made Indian life his study while on earth, and he has endeavoured to render this history, in the touching, descriptive manner, characteristic of the red men of the forests of North America.

THE sun was setting like a globe of molten gold behind the vast prairie of the Far West, which stretched as an illimitable sea in every direction that the eye could reach. One lone spectator of the scene stood upon a rising knoll, covered by high sedgy grass, and scanned the horizon eastward.

This tall, graceful figure, outlined against the evening

sky, was the form of an Indian brave; a blanket, draped in careless folds, hung about his athletic form, and in his listening attitude, full of intuitive grace, he looked like some primeval god,—his handsome, dusky countenance lit up by an expression of hope and expectancy.

Presently his vigil was rewarded by the appearance in the distance of an emigrant waggon, which soon lengthened out into a long train, dotting the far-off horizon with numerous horses and white-covered waggons. As it gradually approached nearer to where the Indian stood, he buried himself in the high grass, creeping upon his hands and knees.

Finally when the train reached the point where he lay hidden, and passed on beyond, he arose and silently followed the travellers. They toiled on westward to where the sun dipped low beneath the prairie, and the ground began to change its aspect as they proceeded.

They were evidently seeking for water, and a spot whereon to encamp for the night. Half-an-hour's further travel and they came upon one of those oases common to prairie land —a little belt of timber, where they halted; and immediately the stalwart pioneers released the jaded horses from their loads, while the women and children began to dismount cheerily from the long covered waggons. Busy hands untied the coarse unbleached coverings, and all the appurtenances of a household were revealed—chairs and stools, kettles and pails, cups and dishes, pans and pots: all betokened the lively household and thrifty family.

The occupants of one of these tent-like waggons appeared far superior to the rest. The head of this family, unlike his ruddy fellow-companions, was a pale, intellectual-looking man, evidently a teacher or preacher, who had left his ill-paid occupation in some crowded city to seek a home and inspiration in the Far West.

This party consisted of his wife, his mother, and a daughter, a young girl of seventeen, one of the most beautiful beings the sun ever shone upon. She possessed an open face, dark eyes, and nut-brown hair; but the beauty of her countenance lay in its expression, which was almost radiant, and caused the beholder to be drawn to her as people are drawn toward sunlight.

While her companions were busy making a fire and preparing the evening's repast, she sat for a time upon the end of the waggon, and looked out in a sort of entranced reverie over the prairie.

She could not see the eyes that were watching her with savage admiration. They were the eyes of the young brave, whom we have described as following so stealthily the caravan, now fixed with mute adoration upon her. Not till she had descended from her position and joined her mother in girlish activity, to prepare their evening gipsy meal, did the Indian brave cease to watch her movements. At length, with a sadness which, had he been a white man, would have found relief in a deep sigh, he turned slowly, all unseen, and crept stealthily away.

As the night gathered over the camp, this lone band of emigrants divided themselves into companies to watch during the long hours of darkness, and prevent any sudden attack from secreted Indians, their dreaded foe. But alas! there was a foe more to be dreaded than the red man, of which this unsuspecting company had not the faintest warning.

Meanwhile Deerfoot—for that was the name of the young Indian brave—hastened to his lodge, some miles distant from the encampment of the emigrants. In the Indian camp he found all in a state of excitement at the arrival of the strangers, for other scouts had been abroad and discovered the emigrant train, and had reported its position to the warriors and chiefs of the Indian band. As night advanced they gathered around the council fire, and eager discussions arose about the new comers. Should they permit them to pass unmolested? or should they run off their valuable cattle, and plunder their waggons?

Deerfoot, sitting on the ground, with his head buried in his hands, listened silently to their plans and projects. At length he spoke:—

"Chiefs and warriors! the Great Spirit has spoken to me; He has looked upon me with an angry eye, while the sun went down over the great prairie; He talked to me of the pale-faces, and said, 'Touch not these men and maidens. They have kindled their fires under My sky; they repose under the shadow of My hand; they trust in Me even as the wild fawn of the forest trusts in its dam.' Brothers, the Great Spirit has spoken. Listen!"

These mystical words of Deerfoot had a strange effect upon the warriors, who grunted in Indian-like fashion their acknowledgment and approbation of his speech.

The night passed quietly, and the lone stars of heaven took their stations and watched peacefully over the encamped strangers, as well as over the lodges of the savages.

The morning dawned with summer-like warmth. The emigrants, wearied by their long march, determined to remain in their well-watered camp a few days to recruit their tired horses, and recover from the fatigue of the past week. That bright morning, all were astir and happy at the present termination of their pilgrimage. Kettles swung above the cheerful fires, and the delicious odour of coffee arose above, and mingled with the fragrance of the flowery prairie.

Breakfast over, the men looked after their several harness and waggon gear, while the elder women repaired garments, and the young girls hunted for berries and flowers, which grew in abundance upon the green slopes and along the river-side; for a stream of water ran along the belt of timber, and the ground, gradually sloping toward the water, was studded with flowers of almost every colour and shape.

Around this glorious *parterre* the waggons were drawn in a semicircle, and the young people were permitted to wander at will in this new Garden of Eden. The beautiful girl who had attracted Deerfoot's attention the night previous, seemed to be followed with girlish admiration by her companions; for every now and then some voice called out, "Oh, Lulu! look at this flower!" or, "Lulu, see this bird!" as one curiosity after another attracted their attention; and they thus attested their friendship for their lovely companion by desiring her to partake of their pleasure.

The sun had ascended high in the heaven, and it was past noon when the hungry girls returned to the camp,— Lulu bearing an apronful of flowers, which she spread before her mother. The delicate woman looked with a sad smile upon her child, as she displayed her floral offerings.

"Ah, my child," said she, caressing her daughter's lovely cheek, "I wish we were back home again, and that I could see the flowers in my little garden. There they were more precious to my eye than these gay blossoms; somehow their bright colours look treacherous. I fear the future for us both, Lulu!"

"Oh, mama, you are tired with your long journey; think of what a pleasant home we will have by-and-by. Then I will plant these brilliant flowers in our new garden. Is not this splendid?" said she, turning up a red spray and twining it in her mother's hair. "I must seek more of it by-and-by, after I have rested. I must go this afternoon, and dig up a large quantity, to plant in a box, and carry with us for our new garden!"

Her mother smiled sadly, and replied: "I am glad to see you so happy, Lulu, but my heart is heavy."

"I will gather more of these red tassels to cheer you up," said the girl; and after the heat of the day had passed, she started off in quest of her prize. She wandered a long distance from the camp, by the water-side, and having found a bed of the flowers she was seeking, was in the act of digging up the roots, when a strange, unaccountable feeling caused her to look up, and there, leaning against the trunk of a tree, she beheld the Indian whom we have described as Deerfoot, standing, with folded arms, watching her earnestly.

Startled, she arose; her first thought was to run, but something in his movement arrested her step, while Deerfoot put out his hands imploringly, and spoke. She could not understand his language, but his musical, pleading tone quieted her fears; her heart interpreted the sound; its tone was that of a mother quieting her child's fears.

"Do not run from me, Lone Star," he said; "thou art more beautiful than all the flowers of the prairie! Listen to me: the cruel hunter is on thy trail! Deerfoot will save thee; he has a strong arm and fleet foot; he will carry thee away safe from the scalping knife."

Of this jargon the maiden understood not a word, but she saw before her a handsome youth, with kindling eye, and love on his tongue, addressing her with soft accent. She comprehended this much: she knew that he was pleased with her appearance, and she, in turn, admired the handsome form and elevated, refined countenance of the brave.

He stooped, and gathering a bunch of pale flowers, offered them to Lulu. She had heard dreadful stories of the Indians, and her chief thought was that she must not vex him. She feared, though he looked so kind, he might prove treacherous, so tremblingly she put out her hand, and accepted his tribute.

Upon that the Indian smiled and placed his hand upon his heart, and she comprehended thereby that a treaty of friendship was made between them. Without language, other than the language of Nature, she understood the compact, bowed, and commenced to retreat.

At this Deerfoot grew excited, and, gesticulating rapidly, he pointed off, as to some distant point. In vivid pantomime he made her understand her camp was in danger of being attacked. Blanched with fear, she listened and watched his tell-tale movements! As soon as he saw that she comprehended him, he retreated back to the shadow of the tree where she had first seen him. He then indicated that the conference was over, and that she might depart.

Breathlessly she hastened to the encampment, the pale flowers he had offered her clutched in her bloodless fingers. Panting, she reached the spot where her mother sat, and threw herself wildly before her.

"Oh, mama! the Indians, the Indians!" she cried. Soon the news spread throughout the camp that they were discovered by the Indians, and would likely be attacked!

Preparations were immediately made by the leaders of the company to intrench their camp, and protect the women and children, if possible, from the onslaught of the expected foe.

But it was not of the savages that Deerfoot had warned Lulu, but of white men, more bloody and savage in their desire for plunder than the red man,—the Christianised white man, who would prove a more terrible enemy than the savage of the forest. Already had certain reckless members of a Mormon settlement approached the Indian camp of which Deerfoot was a member, with whom they were on friendly terms, soliciting their assistance in attacking this large body of emigrants and plundering their camp.

Religious fanatics have ever proved themselves to be more remorseless than savages, and in this case they fairly outdid the much-reviled red man.

By a well-devised plan, disguised as Indians, they attacked the encampment; but the defenders were strong men, and fought bravely to protect their wives and children. The attacking party were few in numbers, having failed to secure the help of the Indians; and not desiring to risk their own precious lives, it was necessary that they should resort to stratagem to disarm this numerous band and gain possession of their cattle and household goods. Accordingly they gave the besieged to understand that if they left their encampment and marched out unarmed, hostilities would cease.

The harassed band gladly acquiesced in the demand. They had lost many of their brave companions in the affray, and with credulous faith worthy of a better fate, they laid down their weapons, and prepared to leave the protection of their encampment.

Lulu, as the most beautiful and courageous of the young girls, was selected to carry in advance the flag of peace. The hapless band, with renewed hope saw her set forth, attired in pure white; her mother, pallid and trembling with forebodings, followed despairingly. Lulu encouraged her with the thought that the Indians, seeing their defenceless condition would befriend them.

But alas for human hopes and intuitions! They had to deal with wolves in sheep's clothing!—with men who combined the cruelty of the Indian with the intelligence of the whites. These creatures knew that they must not leave one alive to tell the tale of their misdeeds.

It was early morning; Deerfoot had left his lodge to seek the encampment of Lone Star, the beautiful maiden, who seemed to him to be an angel of light. What was his horror, as he advanced across the prairie, in the direction of the camp, to see a band of apparent Indians, with rifles and tomahawks in hand, ruthlessly attacking and slaying the white men and women of the encampment he was about to visit!

With steps more fleet than the deer, he hastened toward the place of conflict, inspired by love and awakened by courage. Alas! he was too late! The grass was wet with blood, and in every direction men and women lay slaughtered.

With a wild Indian yell he called aloud for Lone Star, as he rushed among the dead and dying. A low moan from a heap of white drapery at length attracted his attention. He hastened to it, and stooping down beheld the almost lifeless form of Lulu, the Lone Star white maiden whom he was seeking.

With a cry of joy he caught her up in his arms, and fled over the battle-field, carrying his precious burden. On, on he ran, until he reached a stream of water. There he paused bathed her face, and wet her pallid lips with the refreshing draught. She opened her eyes as the cooling water touched her lips, and smiled—a sad, heart-rending smile—as she beheld him. That woful smile entered his soul, leaving an impression that years and death could not efface!

A canoe lay moored by the side of the stream; gathering some leaves, he placed them in the canoe, and tenderly upon them he laid the dying girl.

Then he seated himself beside her, and paddled silently

down the stream. "Lone Star," said he, bending over her, pityingly, "the Great Spirit has appeared to me from the Happy Hunting-grounds. He has told me to carry you to the Beautiful Isles; there you will be happy; there you will be free from pain; there is no war-path there, and death never enters; the Indian brave never raises his war-whoop there. Deerfoot has taken a solemn oath to the Great Spirit that he will avenge the death of your father, and mother, and companions. The Great Spirit has heard his vow; the treacherous white man shall not enter his Happy Hunting-ground till this evil deed has been avenged."

As he closed this adjuration the Angel of Death came for Lulu! With a radiant smile she stretched out her arms, and was borne to the Beautiful Island in the Spirit-land, just as her dusky lover had moored his frail barque against the shore of the island he was seeking for her shelter.

It was a lovely spot in the midst of the water. He lifted the lifeless form upon the grassy bank, and laid it beneath the shade of a tree.

Poor Deerfoot! He was unskilled in the refinements of civilisation, but no white man ever grieved more for the loss of his heart's mistress than did this Indian brave lament the death of Lulu. She became to him a Star in heaven. Upon this lone island he erected her grave in Indian fashion.

He believed that he could not join her in Spirit-land until her murderers were given up to justice. With this belief he soon imbued his tribe.

For a long time the public supposed that the massacre of the emigrants was the work of the Indian tribe. They were aware of this rumour, and knew how falsely they were stigmatised.

At their council fires Deerfoot told his people, in his

eloquent manner, that they must clear themselves from this accusation of shedding innocent blood,—that they could never be happy in the Spirit-land with this stigma resting upon them. He told them that Lone Star, his pale bride, was waiting for him on the Beautiful Island, in the Happy Hunting-ground, and that he could not join her while the red man was held guilty of luring her and her people to destruction.

Possessed with this idea, he mingled with the traders who visited their station, and became through them acquainted with the English language, persistently studying it until he grew so perfect in its use that he could act as interpreter to his tribe. From this time he gave up his occupation as warrior, and grew silent and moody, bent on one purpose—that of delivering up to justice the principal instigators and actors in the terrible massacre.

Finally, by years and years of perseverance, he accomplished his purpose. The whites grew to believe that they had misjudged the Indians, and that some degenerate Latter-day Saints and false Christians, who had grown rich on the spoils of the slain, were the real perpetrators of the crime.

At length the ringleader was brought to justice, and condemned to be executed. Deerfoot, now advanced in years, dressed himself in holiday attire, and stole forth across the prairie to the well-known river, down which he had borne his beloved years agone. With strange joy he stepped into his canoe and set it afloat down the stream toward the Beautiful Isle.

The hour he had been waiting for was at hand; he was to join his Spirit-bride! The excitement which had upheld him for so many years was past. The atonement was made! Already the executioners of justice had sent the chief criminal to meet his final award.

No food had touched the lips of the avenging Indian for forty-eight hours; the long fast, his age, and the enthusiastic belief that his bride was calling him, hastened his death.

As the sun set over the waters surrounding the Beautiful Island the spirit of Deerfoot arose through space to seek his pale bride, Lone Star, in the Island of Bliss, in the World of Spirits.

This is no fancy sketch. Thus often are the real perpetrators of a crime brought to justice by spirit-agency. The light of the Spirit-world reveals all secrets.

PRE-HISTORIC RACE OF MAN.

HERODOTUS.

WHEN the work of producing this volume was begun, the first communication received was from Herodotus, of whom we knew little beyond his name, and certainly had no expectation of receiving a visit from him. The utterances of the spirit were accompanied by objects of antiquity and Oriental scenes, which, in all their wealth and grandeur, flitted past the vision of the clairvoyante. The information communicated by the spirit was as startling and unanticipated as his visit.

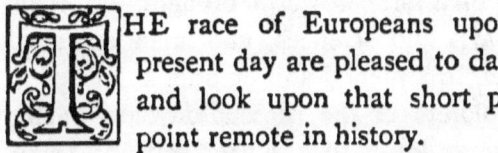HE race of Europeans upon the earth at the present day are pleased to date back 1800 years, and look upon that short period of time as a point remote in history.

Eighteen hundred years back of that is lost in the labyrinth of tradition. Six thousand years has been accredited as the period of the earth's existence, and Bible historians have built up a form of theology upon their supposed data.

Thousands of years before Cheops trod upon the earth, ere Ramesis the Great sat upon his throne, centuries before the supposed period of creation, there lived upon the earth a great nation—a people skilled in art and science.

They were tall in stature with regular features, in appearance between the ancient Greek and Egyptian; they believed in the immortality of the soul, and traced their origin to the gods.

The walls of their great cities are buried beneath the sea. Their temples and monuments are washed by the sands of the ocean. The face of the globe has changed since that day. Great continents have been formed, and the eastern and western hemispheres are divided as they were not at that era.

In the far past, the Spirit-world in its revolution entered into the atmosphere of the material world, and beings from the World of Spirits came upon the earth and dwelt bodily, and brought with them their creative genius, and thus was founded these lost cities.

These inhabitants of a rarefied world brought with them their poetry, their arts and sciences, and man ascended from the animal state, to a mental and emotional one.

The scientific explorers of the present day are tracing man's footsteps from a lower to a higher state of being, but they have yet failed to trace the evolution of the soul from the forces of Nature. The immortal spark which made man the great being that he has proved himself to be in the past—where in Egypt, Syria, Nineveh, and India, and Greece, and the islands of the sea, he has left wonderful tokens of the creative power of the soul—is not an evolution from the lowest germ of matter, but a spark from the great Creative Mind. The humblest animal or bird upon the earth has its brain and nerve connections thereto, which form a battery, and, acted upon by the sun and heat, produces life—motion.

That we call animal life, the life which man possesses in common with the lowest forms of creation. But there is another life, a spiritual life, quickened by a spiritual sun, which animates man, who is the highest form of creation.

The pyramids of Egypt, the object of whose erection has remained a mystery to man, were constructed, for the purpose of communicating with spirits, by the ancestors of these remote people I have spoken of. The great mystery of communicating with spiritual beings by mesmeric passes, and resorting to high mounds or elevations for this intercourse, was a secret in the hands of a few mediumistic and enlightened priests and nobles of that day. Among them the laws of chemical affinities, and the use of certain gases, unknown to-day, and of so-called mesmeric influences, were understood and applied for the purpose of communicating with the Unseen World (but under these conditions it was seen). The mass of men were mere animals, and this science was known only to the learned classes; the mysterious power of communicating with the supernatural world had the effect of stimulating the faculties, and increasing the knowledge, and awakening the higher emotions, and love of the beautiful, even among the uninitiated.

Temples of immense size were erected towering far into the clouds, as a magnet to draw the favourite spirit to that point. All ancient and classic history (so-called) is replete with accounts of spirits appearing to men. In my day it was of such frequent occurrence that no surprise was awakened by it, but the people of whom I speak lived in daily association with the Spirit-world.

All the earlier races of men held belief in pre-existence, and that gods could come down and take possession of the forms of men. The earliest Hebrew records are replete with traditions that angels and gods descended in bodily form, and ate, and talked, and walked, with the patriarchs of old. Long before the days of the Jewish priesthood, spirits walked upon the earth, and intermarried with the inhabitants of earth.

Only among certain races of peculiar physiological development could this advent from the Spirit-world take place.

The ancient Greeks were particularly indebted to the inhabitants of the Spirit-world. Mount Olympus was truly the seat of the gods, as Mount Sinai became in later days the seat or throne of Jehovah. All high mounds are more accessible to spirits. Being lifted from the lower strata of the earth's atmosphere, they are better adapted to the sublimated condition of spiritual visitants.

EXPLORATIONS: ASSYRIAN AND SPIRITUAL.

GEORGE SMITH, ASSYRIOLOGIST.

THE report, which was widely circulated by the newspapers, of a friend of the late George Smith having heard his voice in London while he was absent in the East, raised many speculations as to whether the voice was an intimation of death. George Smith himself unexpectedly communicated, and furnished the following explanation.

S the daily journals have published the fact of my voice having been heard, calling to one of my friends in England, at the moment of my decease, it might prove interesting to my fellow-countrymen to learn how this occurred.

I was engaged in investigating Assyrian remains, and was deeply interested in my work, expecting to take many remarkable examples to England, and add greatly to its historical museum, when suddenly I became ill and died. My first thought, as a spirit, was that I must go to England, which I did, and it is a remarkable fact that I travelled almost as quickly as the thought was formed. How I reached my home I know not, but entering my house, I went to the window to look if any changes had taken place during my absence, and while gazing out, I saw my friend, who was associated with me in my enterprises, passing by at no great distance. My first impulse was to call to him, as I was not conscious of my death, experiencing the same sensations that occur in a dream; but as I called and saw him passing on unheeding me, I partially realised my condition, and as a person with the nightmare strives to scream and be heard, so I struggled frantically, and the effort finally brought him to hear my voice, when he turned in the direction where I stood but saw me not; the vacant air alone met his vision, for he knew not that I was a spirit.

I went hastily to him, but failed to make him comprehend the information I endeavoured to give. I had desired to see him prior to my death, and now we met as strangers, he on one side of the Bridge, and I on the other.

I do not think the sensations experienced by new-born spirits are generally known. No human being can imagine the loneliness felt by a spirit when, like myself, he passes away in a strange land, and returns to his home, and is not recognised.

* * * * *

I have visited the wonderful people whose lost history I was endeavouring to retrace, but have found the truth of the common saying that "distance lends enchantment to the view," for the human mind is so constituted, that it is more interested in discovering that which is out of sight, than in becoming acquainted with that which lies before it. The traveller cares not for the Rome of to-day, it is only ancient Rome that interests him; and though these extinct nations live again in the Spirit-world, yet their broken sculpture and defaced monuments on earth, were of more interest to me than their perfect structures which I have since visited in spirit-life; because, the former are relics of a by-gone race whose history is lost in the obscurity of past centuries, while here the veil is lifted, and I behold them a living people.

It may be valuable to explorers to know that after ascending a certain height from earth, distant objects become clearer, and movements that occur below can be readily discerned by the eye, as verified by recent experiments of aeronauts, who, on ascending a certain distance above the surface, have seen objects distinctly upon earth which would otherwise have been wrapped in obscurity; (as in a well one may see stars that would be invisible to the eye upon the surface of the earth.) I have observed a similar phenomenon as affecting sound, which cannot be heard at a short distance from the earth, but at a given point beyond, it becomes audible.

Thus spirits can hear every note of an opera that is being sung at St. Petersburg, Paris, or London, or at any other point to which they may incline their ear. Spirit-voices are not generally heard on earth owing to the great volume of material sound that daily fills the air. On a still night, upon an open plain, or on a mountain-top, they might be heard if attention were concentrated for that purpose.

* * * * *

I have been told that I was aided in my researches by spirits, which I do not doubt, for I now see that all my co-labourers are thus assisted.

LEAVES FROM MY SPIRIT-JOURNAL.

DR. LIVINGSTONE.

THE attention of the medium was arrested by the appearance of an emaciated and elderly man, who occupied a sitting posture on a litter which was carried by four black men. The spirit thus introduced proved to be the great African traveller, who gave his narrative in a homely and unsophisticated manner. Much that he communicated was in an easy colloquial style, referring to commonplace matters, which have been omitted; hence the interruptions to be observed in his contribution.

I WAS daily growing weaker, so that I could scarcely walk, or hold my pen to note my journey, when my faithful attendants placed me in a little hut sheltered from the sun and winds. * * * Shortly after this I became insensible. * * * Some days elapsed before I became conscious, and aware that I was a spirit. * * * My spirit-friends did not take me immediately from earth, knowing the shock it would give me to be suddenly removed from the land of my adoption, but remained with me while I (as a spirit) accompanied my faithful African followers as they bore my lifeless body through the wild country.

* * * * *

When I had fully regained my strength and vitality, at

my desire my friends conducted me to Central Africa, in the Spirit-world.

This country I found to be some hundreds of years in advance of the corresponding district on earth, and diversified with mountains, rivers, and fertile plains.

Africa here resembles my ideal Africa. Her ancient cities exist again in this world of antiquity; thus history repeats itself.

Those who read this book may wonder why I do not give an accurate description of the unexplored portion of Africa. It is one of the laws of this strange world in which I reside, that no revelation shall be made to man that will interfere with his own investigations. I have opened the way to those who will follow; where my foot failed to tread, others will walk.

Here I would like to offer my thanks to that intrepid young American who braved the dangers of that unknown land to carry aid to the supposed lost traveller. I could not then desert the land of my adoption, nor can I yet, and hope still, unseen by him, as a spirit, to accompany him in further explorations.

* * * * *

Having been informed by my spirit-guides that gorillas possessed a species of soul, and were capable of a spiritual existence, I desired to visit their homes, which I did. I found them living in a region quite by themselves, in close proximity to earth's Africa. They were advanced a little beyond the animal, more like the barbarous tribes of Africa; very large in stature, and seeming to possess their intelligence principally through their intercourse with spirits. They live in huts, and subsist on fruits and grain, are especially friendly, and possessed with affectionate dispositions. I have been told that on earth they had a glimmer of their position, and were unhappy in it.

Though not capable of developing a language, they possessed the power of communicating among each other, to a limited degree, through vocal sounds.

* * * * *

Swedenborg, while in the superior condition, long ago discovered that the African possessed attributes fitted to place him in a very high position in the Spirit-world. His docility of character, his imitativeness, his desire to learn, all fit him to rank high in the scale of being, if opportunity for progression be offered to him.

To me this people became as of my own kindred, and their land became my land. Never will I forget the kindness and hospitality I experienced while travelling in that idolatrous country.

Ah! these children of the Sun are indeed examples to European nations! I will yet see the day, from my starry home, when the country I love will become a cultured garden, and her people among the most intelligent on earth.

I feel it to be a misfortune for a person to be taken from the world before he has accomplished the object of his life.

Thought and desire become intensified in the spiritual condition, and I find it difficult to break away from the scene of my explorations and become equally interested in the Spirit-world.

My great desire on earth was to aid in Christianising Africa, to introduce commerce and the arts into that fertile land. The people are exceedingly mediumistic; their wild superstitions are the result of conditions. Living as they do in scattered tribes and surrounded by wild beasts, fear and ignorance cause them to misunderstand the spiritual appearances, which consequently assume distorted and grotesque shapes to their eyes.

ITALY AND THE CHURCH.

VICTOR EMANUEL.

THE medium was in Paris, November, 1878, when Victor Emanuel suddenly appeared to her. He said he recollected her, that she had bowed to him on the Pincian Hill, and that he always recollected those who saluted him thus. He stated also that he had been that afternoon on the Pincian Hill at Rome. His influence was rather abrupt, but genial. As his communication was given before the attack on Prince Humbert's life, the portion where the king alludes to his son seems verified by subsequent events.

INGS must die, as well as other men. Their earthly power has no control over the realm of spirit. I am now a mere man; once a soldier, next a king, but always a *man*.

Death did not alarm me, for a soldier should always be prepared for a march. I knew something about Spiritism; I believed that spirits could revisit earth; I knew that I should return again as a spirit. My sweet daughter Marguerite is a medium; she sees me often. I can approach her and my son Humbert. Fear not, Italia; my son will act wisely, I will stand beside him to protect and guide.

I had the happiness of welcoming my friend and holy father Pio Nono to the World of Spirits. All is peace between us now; his spirit hailed me with joy: surprised and pleased to find that I was not in Purgatory, but moving about free from the excommunication he placed upon me. He is forced to see the great truth that was given to me to fight for, that Italy belongs to the Papal power only spiritually, as other Catholic countries, and not materially. This her right I will maintain above all principalities and powers, and in this assumption I am sustained by mighty hosts in the World of Spirits. My beloved country occupies my time and fills my mind. I look over the heads of government—seeing, but not seen; ready to ward off all blows that may be directed against her peace and liberty.—Victor Emanuel.

BLESS, AND CURSE NOT!

THE POPE.

THE medium had bought some rosary-strings in Rome, and one day while in Paris, several months after, she thoughtlessly placed a chaplet of amber beads upon her wrist as a bracelet. Suddenly she saw the old Pope as in life, with his long robe and skull-cap upon his head, smiling benignantly upon her; and he then gave the following communication.

✠

ENEDETTISSIMA—I was called PAPA. I have travelled far to see you. You wear an amulet which I blessed; retain it; it will give you strength. "Whatever you bless on earth shall be blessed, and whatever you curse shall be cursed," said the blessed Lord. Impious man says not so. No man has power to curse! Has not the viper power to sting? Are not bad thoughts infectious, and good ones healing? Therefore never curse any man, but bless always, and blessings will return to you. I am rejoiced that I lived long enough on earth to take back my curses and recall my anathema. A father's arms should open wide to the most erring child.

My Cardinals would not permit me to act as I wished to; I was immured in the Vatican; they made me a prisoner. I would have forgiven Italy and Victor Emanuel, and abdicated as head of the State, but I was forced to do the behests of others. Old age brings wisdom and moderation, but youth calls these cowardice and weakness.

How simple are the people of my country! They have gathered portions of my garments as holy relics; even the straw of my bed have they divided amongst themselves to keep them from evil and heal them of disease.

Impotent matter, lifeless and useless, yet possessing a magic power when pervaded by the good wishes of the wearer. This power of imparting healing virtue belongs to many men; it is not a miracle worked only upon holy priests and saints. I see on earth many good men who should be canonized, who belong to all creeds and nations.

The African savage wears his amulet to keep off the Fetish or evil spirit; the true Catholic preserves his relic to draw down the influence of the good spirits or holy saints. In themselves they are valueless; time dissipates their magnetism; but they serve as anchors to concentrate the mind. As it is said, "Only believe and ye shall be saved."

Once more I give my blessing to all. I must go to my dear people in Rome. The Church calls me; my brother, Leo XIII. calls me. Addio. PIO NONO.

TO THE REPUBLIC OF FRANCE.

THIERS.

THIS noble spirit was brought to the medium by a crowd of great Frenchmen, among whom the distinguished Lamartine and Napoleon. As M. Thiers says, it was the anniversary day of his death, and Paris was keenly alive to his soul-influence. He appeared disturbed by the parade and church ceremonies, and expressed himself vigorously.

THE anniversary of my death has been recently celebrated in Paris, and it caused my heart to throb with happiness to see that the Republic had so many good friends on that occasion who showed their honour to it through my manes. I would die a hundred times and make a hundred corpses, if thereby I could discover so many friends to the Republic of France! We have had enough of cockades, enough of the Légion d'Honneur; now let us have sensible Frenchmen. Let the golden vestments that crowned Napoleon rot in Notre Dame; we require only the plain citizen's dress to install our President in office.

To the priests and prelates, who have laboured truly for France and the poor, I make my obeisance; I will dip my fingers in the holy water that they bless; they may light the candles around my catafalque; but for those who connive with princes and politicians to keep the people in darkness and ignorance, I say that I will use my spirit-power in overturning their plots.

Why should men live for mere selfish ends? If they consider the good of the nation above their own aggrandisement, they will be blessed finally. If deposed from power they will be reinstated, as I was, on a more lofty pedestal in the world of immortality!

Lamartine is here, the moving spirit of the age; he hovers around France, and from many a priestly cell, from many an editor's chair, from many a workman's bench, he speaks for the Republicism of France. Down with the aristocracy that would reinstate the Papal power—that would exhaust the wealth of the nation in forging golden crowns and chains to ornament a weak man and tyrant, whose only office would be to control the liberty of the Press and prevent the people demanding what they need for body and soul! Down with the miscreants of the Inquisition! Down with dark ignorance! Spread wide the light of knowledge to enlighten the whole world! Adieu.

EPIC OF A SOUL.

G. H. LEWES.

The medium was residing at the Spiritual Institution, London, and was recovering from an illness, but still weak and lying upon her bed, when she saw a spirit with dark hair, massive brain, and slight body, sitting at a chair before a round table, upon which she had left strewn MSS. He seemed busy with the papers, and would turn and look at her seriously with questioning eyes ever and anon. The next day she saw the same spirit, and placing herself at the table, she was powerfully controlled by the spirit, and gave the following communication, which was written through her hand. Date—March, 1879.

PEOPLE call me a rank Materialist. Perhaps I was one. I did not believe in a God, not, at least, in one made by human hands,—by the imaginings of despotic, tyrannical, changeable man—such as most of my fellow-beings worshipped.

I believed in man using his reasoning faculties, and investigating all abstruse and mysterious matters generally taken on faith; and that if he did so, he would find some natural law to explain all those wonders.

The world was growing out of the blind faith of childhood, into the reasoning state of manhood, and I endeavoured to help its growth. I had seen many idols destroyed; old beliefs had been swept away with the story of Noah's ark and the six days' creation. I had arrived at that point where I would not believe anything that could not be proven—that had not some geological strata, so to speak, to support it; and now the time had come for me to try the *Great Unknown*.

Future existence had never been proven conclusively to my mind, and I had investigated the treasures of Nature till I had arrived at the conclusion that, within her bosom, the beginning and ending of my identical self would cease, or a general absorption would take place into some creative principle.

Darkness was closing around me, the light of life was fading; I felt that I was returning to atomic life—my heart would be stilled for ever. I would feel no more, suffer no more. There was *one* heart that would suffer, but I would not know of it. Nature called me back to the unthinking dust of centuries. I was going from animate matter back to inanimate—that was all. The brain that was then acting would soon cease to vibrate, and thought and remembrance, the result of that mechanical action, would close with it. This was the whole mystery of that last hour!

I reflected thus as life was ebbing away. If I seemed unconscious, I was not. I knew that I was dying, like a wasted fire, and all that would be left of me would be a blackened heap—a handful of ashes.

The dark waves of a shoreless eternity swept over me, and the great blank of my life came . . . But how? was it a conscious blank? I had felt the cold waves of oblivion sweeping over me, but I was washed up by the billows—Where? upon some shore? Yes. Hear it, my friends! hear it! I lived.

Following a few moments of insensibility—I know not how many, but the time seemed short,—I awakened as with an electric shock, and became conscious, as if looking at the sun through water. A yellow, thick glow of atmosphere surrounded me, and I endeavoured to lift up my hand to wipe the cobwebs from my brain; but I seemed to have no hand, no member but my head. I appeared to be a great round ball, emitting light like the sun—that was all! Remembrance I had none; but sensation I experienced. There came to me a feeling as of hearing music, as of smelling the perfume of flowers,—a delicious basking, dreamy sensation of pleasure. I LIVED! Hours went by thus. After a time I came to realise that I could see out through the top of this round ball—this luminous globe which composed the identical *I*. I saw a vast extent of country, with distant purple outline of mountains, and over all a yellow glow. Still, no remembrance of the past troubled me. I do not know how long this state lasted, but after a time I experienced a desire to move, to roll my head. And I commenced to roll it—it was all I had; and as I moved it—slowly at first, but faster and faster afterward—it began to rise up from the ground on which it appeared to lie, to mount upward, and I felt like a boy following his ball,—running over mountain and moon with his *ball*. I was a boy again! That was my first glimpse of memory. I was a boy, and flying through the air, carried onward by my ball, to which I had tied a cord, and let fly through the air, and it was bearing me away! away from home, from all trouble, all fault-finding, all self-complaining, all restrictions. *I was free!*

Oh, how I had striven for freedom! It had come at last! . . . . On, on I moved in spiral lines; higher and higher, like a bird, rapid and more rapid, till I seemed to be suddenly untwining, like a child in a swing; objects became clearer, and lo! I was in a room, a familiar room, and low down, prone in agony, grovelled *one.* I knew her head buried in her hands, her sobs stirring the air, and I went up to her. I knew it all then, as by a flash of light. All the past returned to my memory, and I knew I had left her. I tried to speak to her, to call her by name, to solace her with the knowledge that I was there, *present;* but I could not make her lift up her head. "Oh, my darling! my heart's life! I am not dead!"—I wanted to say, but I could not make her hear. Then came upon my mind a rush of feelings of indescribable misery. I had taught her to believe that I would return to unreflective matter. Could I undo the theory I had built up with such care? Should I be like an idiot, and pull down the corner-stone of my own house? I had taught that man was but the effect of natural causes, and would return back to nature like a rotten tree, when his short life-struggle was over. How could I convince her it was a falsehood, and that I was sensible, and near her.

I am filled with a great sadness to think I did not believe in a hereafter, and arrange with the one who loved me better than I loved myself, to meet my spirit at some trysting place; that I did not bid her select a certain tree or flower, and call upon me, and I would assume its shape, or to fix her eye upon some star in the firmament thinking of me, and I would stand upon one of those glittering points —a living soul.

I am rather a reticent man, not accustomed to reveal my feelings to the gaping crowd; under the guise of fiction I might unburthen my feelings, but I could not show my wounds to a multitude—expose my pierced hands and feet; I had not enough of the Christ principle in me for that. But what does it matter now? I am past the conventionalities of life; I have thrown off my mask. The laws and rules that hampered me on earth do not reach me here. I am amenable to other laws; and for one who gave her life for me, who sacrificed for me and suffered for and with me untold bliss and agony—for her I am writing; I see no one but herself. My reputation is nothing to me now; and the thought of what the world of letters will think of me for writing in this free manner does not disturb me. I am in the world of souls, and soul is speaking to soul, and heart to heart. I burn with a frenzied desire to make her hear me, feel me, see me as a living spirit.

Oh, if the fossils only could speak, what would they say? I am a fossil; I feel as if I had lived before the flood, and the tide of waters had lifted me up upon this high mountain and left *her* down low in the plain, and she would not hear me, or could not, and was turning to stone before my eyes. Oh, my love, hear me! Use your noble powers to behold my revivified being.

I am coeval with all life,—with the mastodon, and the megatherium, and the polype,—with nature in all her stages of progress.

I understand Zoroaster and Pythagoras, Plato and Socrates; the gods of Egypt and Asia, and the deities of Greece and Rome. I comprehend all languages. How childish seem the abstruse thoughts over which I puzzled my brain on earth! I *live* and *love;* that sums up all my life at present. What greater happiness can befall a soul?

Do I live in the air or in the sea, in a house or in a cave? I know not. In certain conditions of the mind we know not locality; in the first moments of grief, or of love, or of hate, we take no cognizance of where we are. But I shall soon begin to use my reflective faculties. As yet all the affairs of life seem unimportant: its misunderstandings, its conjectures, and assertions alike are valueless. All the questions that puzzled me on earth take their place with antediluvian nature; while I soar here a free spirit in this upper world, *the Next World*. I will have a new chart engraved, and Humboldt and Descartes, Goethe and Strauss, Comte and Shakespeare, Lyell and Newton, shall each write a chapter for my new "Annals of Creation," my "Footsteps of Infinity," "The Record of a Human Soul's Rise from Materiality to Eternal Life."

This atmosphere seems to deaden my analytic powers, and I only seem capable of flying back and forth, from those I love in one world to those I love in another. The rest I could never find on earth I find here.

Dry the tears from your eyes, my love, and mount with me in soul; I will take you to a quiet spot where one I loved in childhood has a home. It is real, and yet it appears like a dream; long sweeping branches of trees droop over that spot, and there are quiet dales and sunny uplands there, and a perfume like the breath of God permeates the place.

Come with me, my love. I am young again; all the frailties of life have only helped to bring our feet here. We will bury the fossils of the past—all the records of Fetish worship, all the idols of false religion, of mock adoration, all the Church dogmas which stifle the conscience with words—we will forget them all. We have done a good work, we have helped to knock down the rotten timbers which sustained a false god; now we will rebuild, and teach the *Ego* individualised and indestructible.

It is not I who am talking, it is *her* soul speaking through me. I find myself sitting here at this table beside this strange lady, talking, I do not know how or by what means. Do you think I would talk thus through every medium, as they are called? No; but she has thoughts and feelings like the *one* I love, and she draws my thoughts from me as the Æolian harp draws the sad voice of the wind and repeats it.

She does not force me to feel that I must be punished for having been a Materialist—that I must grope through darkness before I come to the light: punishment has no part in her nature.

I have tried to speak elsewhere, and the people made me feel so abject, so dark, that I gave it up; for the soul takes on the thoughts and feelings around it, and is represented more or less truthfully by the medium through which it has to pass. This lady's mind is in harmony with mine; but if I had to materialise my spirit through some mediums I have visited, I would come out an Indian with his tomahawk, for such would be my mood, and the savage, destructive attribute of my spirit is all I could manifest through some individuals. But through this lady I give utterance to soul thoughts. I feel to be DOUBLE—myself and one dear to me who lingers yet on earth—and it is *her* grief and *her* despairing soul that speaks, through and with me, this rhapsody. Do what you like with it—burn or publish—it has been a strange satisfaction to me to speak, to write.

You make a thing wrong by teaching that it is wrong. If a child be told that it is wicked to pluck the flowers blooming in the garden, he will feel like the very devil for doing so; but, remember, it is the angels who have taught him that the flower is beautiful, with its lovely colours, its soft petals, and delicious perfume! and you go against the God in him when you teach him it is wrong.

Well, I gathered flowers where I ought not, and sheltered wounded birds that I ought to have left to perish, if human theory be right. But I am comparatively safe now from censure; and, like Jack's beanstalk, I have pushed through the earth into the sky in one short night.

Oh, immortal tale of infancy! thou hast a soul-wide significance. I have fought the giants of Doubt and Materiality, and the palace of Infinite Life is before me to wander through.

CHRISTIANITY AND SPIRITUALISM.

WILLIAM HOWITT.

SHORTLY after the death of Mr. Howitt, the medium resided for a few weeks at the Spiritual Institution. Mr. J. Burns had only met Mr. Howitt once, and had not corresponded with him very frequently, as they occupied somewhat different spheres of thought. He was all the more surprised that the presence of the deceased gentleman should haunt him continually; and a warm feeling of regard sprang up within his breast, actuating him to do something in remembrance of the veteran's worth. Without any mention of this being made to the medium, William Howitt presented himself to her with a serene and happy countenance, saying he was in company with George Thompson, G. H. Lewes, and others. The communication was accidentally interrupted, and though continued at another sitting, it was with some difficulty and hesitation, as the spirit seemed at a loss what to state and what to withhold. To meet the expectations of his many friends, he hoped he would find other channels of communication soon, and add to what he was unable to conclude on that occasion.

ERE, in this pleasant sunny room, surrounded by tranquilising influences, I feel at home; for it is neither fine furniture nor costly pictures that make a room congenial to refined and progressed spirits, but it is the harmonious atmosphere that pervades

it. I have been brought hither to furnish a communication for "The Next World." I have known James Burns, the editor of *The Medium and Daybreak*, many years, and also by reputation. Now I know him face to face as a spirit. In him I perceive a more outspoken and energetic labourer for the truth of spirit-communion than I was. Every progressive man, I believe, is born, symbolically speaking, with a renovating instrument in his hand. One wields a pick-axe, and he has to strike hard blows; another a shovel or spade, and he digs at the roots of evil; another has a scythe, and mows right and left; I was born with a small pruning-knife wherewith to lop off the dead branches. The editor of the *Medium* is like one of the newly-invented reaping-machines which cuts through the grain, and piles it up on one side ready to bind; he classifies and brings together all the straggling sheaves, and endeavours to place all into one sheaf—one society.

Every man has an appointed place to fill, and must labour with the instrument he possesses. For me Spiritualism proved a great boon, as it harmonised all the inexplicable mysteries of Nature and Revelation. I think it is better, to live in a peaceful and sunny vineyard, than to destroy the vines because they are a little diseased; it is better to prune than to cut down. I found Christianity like a sheltering vine with many crooked and rotten limbs, but I would prune them and *not destroy*. Harmony and equality are what I would plead for in life.

Whoever makes Bible history his study, cannot but perceive the fact, that, Spiritualism and Christianity are identical in spiritual phenomena. Take this passage: "When the doors were shut, came Jesus and stood in the midst," just as I now appear to this medium. She sees me, with my accustomed visage, just as Peter, and Thomas, and John saw

Christ. I have written about haunted houses and apparitions, and now my ghost is haunting this medium till my work is done, in the same manner that Shakespeare (medium that he was) described the ghost of Hamlet's father. The medium feels a nervous twinge when I approach, as all spiritual visitors cause people to feel. I find that every thinking person wishes to know something about his future life. I can liken this life to nothing but an Italian sunset, when earth and heaven respond and meet, and the one enhances the beauty of the other.

In Rome, where I spent the latter years of my life, we have in the Sistine Chapel a terrible picture called "The Last Judgment;" it is an exponent of the Christian religion as taught and believed by its advocates, an exhibition of the most fearful woes conceivable being inflicted, upon human beings after death, by the great Judge of heaven and earth; a picture to make a man cross himself and shudder. In past times as I have looked upon that painting I have thought, Can it be possible any future state indicates a condition such as this supposed inspired painter has here de-depicted? I expect to converse with Michael Angelo and Dante about their works.

But I have found nothing akin to that condition in the summer-like harmony which pervades all around me, and yet there are spheres or rings of comparative inharmony: states like Mount Vesuvius, being in a half seething condition, that now and again eject fire and smoke. The spiritual condition is emblemised by the material one. I find a remarkable correspondence between the material and spiritual states.

When I state that it is all peace and harmony here, I mean where I am habitually; but I have made incursions down in the lower states, and there I have found almost every condition that has been described in the Bible and books of inspiration. I have seen men going about seeking whom they could devour spiritually; ignorant, half-savage spirits who haunt and molest men, devoting their attention especially to those who are unacquainted with, or opposed to, spirit-communion.

It is best to have some Christ to pray to, some guardian saint to call upon, who can protect from these mischievous influences. But a belief in Christ, and the intercession of saints, does not avail in many cases, because people take only one phase of Christ's character to dwell upon in their thoughts, and so, fail to reach his sphere of existence. Man should hold himself free to receive good from every source.

If a person wishes to go wrong he will find numberless spirits willing to undertake to lead him thereto. This spirit life is an anomaly. Some spirits can assume almost any shape they choose to, because they understand the properties of matter; they can draw out of the elements of Nature phantom shapes of flowers, trees, houses, horses, dogs, or with whatever they can superinduce a spiritual *rapport*.

The medium sees me in my own proper shape, according to the elements I gathered together on earth, but I could gather other properties and assume another appearance.

This science of transmutation and transmigration is better understood by spirits of a more mechanical and inventive genius, than by myself, or those of which I am a type.

It is only by educating and developing man's capacities that he can subdue disorderly spirits, as it is only by educating his higher phrenological attributes that the lower propensities can be subjected: as in the natural world, while the earth becomes more highly cultivated, the gross animal forms gradually disappear.

Swedenborg was a great seer and has described accurately conditions which I have found here, but he has wrongly interpreted them.

Mr. G. H. Lewes, who is present, says he would like to write upon this subject.

Unhappy spirits do not disturb me, because I do not fight them, but speak kindly and persuasively to them. Humanity is alike in Spirit-world as on earth. The wild savage can be tamed by kindness, but not by the sword. Do not explore unknown seas without a chart. I wish to say to my family and friends, Do not fear to take the voyage I have taken with *my chart.*

I did what I could for humanity, and am rewarded here. Do not misunderstand me and think that I advocate religious shackles; I merely would advise that the freed slave should not turn upon his master and cut him down, but should bask in the warmth of his love, and receive the protection he offers.

This is the attitude I advise Spiritualists to take toward Christianity. I am not a leader, as I said in the beginning; I can only point out the evils, and help to prune them away.

I shall labour for the cause of spiritual truth and the progress of humanity as I ever have done, unheeding the bickerings and perversions of factions.

Truth rises grandly above all inferior conditions; gold must always have its alloy. The aims of mankind are so far below what they should be, and the reformer has to lead on such an undisciplined host, that I rejoice I have ceased my labours as a material being, and commenced them as a spiritual one.

A CALL TO FREEDOM.

GEORGE THOMPSON.

THIS spirit was present on several occasions during the last days of the medium's residence at the Spiritual Institution, desirous of sending a message to those on earth. The clairvoyant medium described him as a "tall, military, gentlemanly spirit," who gave the name of George Thompson; but she seemed not to recognise him or be acquainted with his history. Princess Alice was giving her communications, and when she could not use the conditions any further Z. J. Pierart controlled for a short time, speaking in French, and recognising Mr. Burns (the publisher) whom, through the medium, he warmly shook by the hand. George Thompson was the next spirit to manifest. He delivered his speech in a commanding, eloquent manner, with appropriate gesture. He commenced by making a personal allusion to the gentleman just named, who acted as amanuensis. George Thompson will be recognised by many as the eloquent champion of the anti-slavery movement, and was for some time Member of Parliament for the Tower Hamlets.

E are both labourers in the cause of Freedom. I laboured to break the fetters of the slave; you labour to break the bands of old tradition that hold the world enslaved.

It is commonly said that when a man dies his work is done; but I am happy to say that remark will not prove true in my case, for I intend to fight for the good cause till there is not a slave left upon the earth, of any kind, moral or physical.

I see many evils to be remedied, many bonds to be broken. Though England, I am proud to say, has stood forth as an example to the world—a pioneer of Freedom—yet she has lowered her standard, she has draggled it through blood, and the slavery she disowns on one side she fosters on the other.

Now have I to take my stand against the warfare which she is waging with unhallowed zeal—a warfare which will enslave those nations, and crush beneath her triumphant heel all the instincts of manhood from the peoples. But her march is onward, civilisation follows in her wake, and the Spirit-world holds such a dominant power over her that she will be arrested in her bloody march, and plant the ensign of Peace and Progress amid all the savage nations of the earth.

An immense multitude of freed slaves, led by the anti-slavery leaders of the past, welcomed me to the shores of the Summerland. It is good, when a man's work is done, to reap the reward of it. On earth we plant and water the soil, and often look vainly for the tardy crop; but in the Spirit-world we behold the harvest. There it is, all ripe to our hand; we have just to go in and gather it.

I cannot talk more. The medium is used up; all the power has gone; say for me what I cannot say for myself.

[The amanuensis expressed the pleasure it gave him to hear from an old friend whom he so highly esteemed; and in a tone of sadness uttered a word of regret at the indifferentism which at present paralyses the moral energies of mankind. The spirit proceeded.]

People are indifferent because they cannot see what we see. They do not realise their own conditions. You must unrivet the chains from the too-willing slave. No one likes to have applied to himself the term "slave," but all who are in moral darkness and cling to that condition are slaves; and those who are free, and do not put forth their hands to help others, are worse than slaves, because they do not use the light they have.

But there will be a great stirring up of the dry bones soon. Those who are indifferent and selfishly thoughtless of the needs of those around them, will be made to arise up, as by a mighty wind, and be forced to scatter of their abundance in all directions.

AN APPEAL ON BEHALF OF CHILDREN.

PRINCESS ALICE.

THE medium was on the eve of leaving England, and was exhausted by a day of much literary activity. The Princess Alice had been seen several times about the rooms of the Spiritual Institution, apparently anxious to communicate. It was not intended that any other spirits should give their experiences, but out of regard for the Princess the best conditions available were gladly placed at her disposal. The medium was put into the mesmeric state by her attendant spirits, when one of them, an Indian girl, described a "very nice lady" present, accompanied by three children, two girls and one boy, who gave the name of Alice. That spirit then spoke the following sentences through the medium, with rather rapid utterance, and in a dignified manner; and appeared to recognise other spirits in the room as she went along.

I HAVE returned to the land of my birth to thank the subjects of my august mother for the kind words and thoughts they have given me in the hour of my departure from this sphere of earthly joy and sorrow.

My noble father had been looking for me; long has he waited for the presence of some of his beloved family. I and my dear children have been selected to join him. I humbly bow before that Supreme Power that hath awarded me this happiness. We are united now.

I find that I have ever been guided by bright spirits; for they led me to those works of charity which have been lauded as my own acts.

My maternal love is strong, and I am gratified with having a portion of my little family with me in the Spirit-world. I opened my heart to all the world, and from this moment I dedicate myself specially to the work of watching over the asylums for infants and homeless children that are established in this land and in the land of my adoption.

Bright bands of spirit-children welcomed us on our arrival in Spirit-land. Recently another beautiful angel of our household, I may so say, has joined our group, and will become another member of the *Kinder-Garten* which I have established. Those little spirits desire me to speak of the feast which we are preparing for them in the beautiful *Kinder-Garten.*

[The spirit could no longer control, and the delivery of the forgoing remarks was interrupted with long pauses. "Janie," a little girl in spirit-life who frequently controls the medium in the trance, now spoke for a short time, alluding to this children's feast, to which she said she was invited, and, like all children with such a prospect in view, was highly delighted. She said the Princess Alice desired further to say that she hoped the *Kinder-Garten* system of education for the young would be adopted more generally on earth. Children should not be made to learn by rote without being able to perceive the meaning attached to their lessons; but they should be taught by objects and actions, symbolical of principles of life which they naturally represent, and accordingly could be easily remembered by.]

April, 1879.

PHILOSOPHY:
ANCIENT AND MODERN.

RALPH WALDO EMERSON.

THE Medium, after three years' residence in her American home, returned to England, May, 1882. The first spirit to present himself in her new abode was Emerson, whose recent departure to the Spirit-world, caused a wave of thought to be directed from earth to this unique Transcendentalist. The communication is full of thought, and is decidedly Emersonian. It should be read carefully, as it unveils a grand truth.

EMBERS of the Cambridge School of Philosophers are disappearing from sight. Eclipsed on the earthly side of vision, they shine with a resplendent glory on the Spiritual Side.

Shall I claim to have belonged to that School, or to have founded any school of thought? No! I merely reflected the ideas of the Athenian Philosophers—of the Sages of past ages.

The thinkers who existed before the Christian Era have been resurrected in this age, re-incarnated in certain individuals; and what I taught of truth, was not the truth of to-day, but the truth that sprang into existence thousands of years ago; which, like the corn buried with the Egyptian mummies—lying dormant two thousand years, yet retaining its life-principle—finding, in the Nineteenth Century, a suitable soil, on being planted after its long sleep in catacombs, springs up and flowers; and thus again is the food that germinated before the Christian Era given to the world.

My mind having proved a suitable soil, I was thus enabled to re-incarnate ancient thoughts to the reader of the Nineteenth Century.

I trace clearly now the sources of my inspiration. The great mystery of life, its paradox, complex action of thought and cross purposes; how broad, liberal ideas are eliminated from narrow, puritanic teachings, by interchange of thought between the two worlds: I should rather say spirit, because not only the *thought* of the spirit, but the spirit itself becomes embodied temporarily in the individual with whom it assimilates.

Man, spiritually, is a great infant, a child in arms. He does not understand the first principle of the life that sustains him. His true relation to the Spirit-world is as a child to its mother, and he is sustained, fed, and nourished by that mother, although not comprehending the source from whence he derives his sustenance. But he, in his pride of intellect, assumes to think his own thoughts, to create them independent of spirit-agency, while the philosopher will reflect that his best thoughts come to him when, with the simplicity of a child, he abandons himself to the silent teachings of the World of Spirits.

Ideas gathered from the outside world, have to be withdrawn into the spiritual hive, ere the honey can be compounded from them.

The reward is double to him who can receive truths and utter them again. The Spirit-world is open to him who has the capacity to receive it.

Unfoldment is the work of individual effort, and also of natural endowment. He who labours to obtain knowledge will immediately draw aid from spiritual sources, which the indifferent cannot attain. Schools of Philosophy should teach individuals to labour after spiritual knowledge, which comes not only through a passive state of receptivity, but through brain travail and study of the best thought of all ages. The Next World is not a commercial world. It is a world of ideas. Those who wish to enter a happy state there, should develop their mental and spiritual powers.

It is not given to anyone to teach all truth. The thoughts that I gave to the world have returned to me a hundredfold. The effort of each mind should be to keep free from erroneous and dogmatic teachings, unbiassed by narrow creeds, by dark and morbid pictures of the Unknown. By free interchangings of ideas, conversaziones which will permit unpremeditated utterances, you will receive intelligence from the Athenian Philosophers, from the scholastic Egyptians, and from the great Universe of Spirit.

EMERSON.

THE POLITICAL SITUATION IN ENGLAND.

LORD BEACONSFIELD.

On the day succeeding the anniversary of his demise, Beaconsfield appeared. The Medium saw him clearly. He was dressed with care: his countenance pale, but happy in expression. He spoke, as a diplomatist, with caution and deliberation. Cavendish, the Irish Secretary, and Burke, victims of the assassin, were in his company.

KIND FRIENDS,—Did you ever look through a diminishing glass to find yourself reduced to a tenth of your size, and represented as ill-favoured and ill-formed? One's vanity is apt to be shattered by such a view of one's personality. Since I left the earth I have been in a position analogous to a person looking through a diminishing glass.

I rode on the top wave of popularity: the Prime Minister of England and Privy Counsellor of the Queen, honoured for the moment; the literary curiosity, applauded as a giant in intellect; as a courtier, a favourite of fortune, and one whom the gods delighted to honour.

From this exalted position I suddenly was thrust down. The smiles of kings and princes, the applause of the multitude were withdrawn, and thus my life was an epitome of all life. I took the lesson that was taught me silently, and again turned my attention to literature; here, said I, man may become immortal; here public favour is enduring, and does not applaud one day and stab its victim the next.

But I had one more lesson to learn. Another change occurred in my horoscope. The star of my life set on earth to rise dimly in another Sphere of existence. And now, from this Cloud Land, I look through the diminishing atmosphere between the two worlds, to find that my *mirage* on earth is reduced to a mere speck. Triumphant chariot-wheels cover up the tracks where I once walked; the pale primroses of spring are the only mementoes that are left of Beaconsfield.

And what a lesson of the mutations of life! A lesson that should be studied by all popular favourites, who live on the breath of the multitude.

My fame rose like a bubble that sparkled in the sunlight— like a bubble it burst, and scattered the hopes it had raised.

Seldom in England's history has she stood more in need of a wise head and a strong heart to direct her course than to-day. A vulture is gnawing at her vitals, and will destroy her unless it is itself destroyed.

An aggregation of power ever has a tendency to destroy the very foundations upon which it is built. My policy, while Premier of England, was to strengthen the nation which I served, not by oppressive means, but by stretching out the friendly, strong, and jewelled hand in all directions; by dispensing wealth, and the emblems of wealth; by displaying munificence with power. I desired that England might resemble the great Jewish kingdom prophesied of in history, and extend from the rising to the setting of the sun.

The policy of the present English Government towards Ireland, is a question that now deeply interests the inhabitants of the Spiritual Spheres.

I believe in a strong government, and in holding the reins firmly, but they should be so held (if I may liken the subjects to a steed), that the steed feels as if acting his own pleasure, and is not coerced. The hand that holds a dagger should ever be kept from sight.

Not only England, but all the kingdoms of the earth are to be stirred from their foundations. In saying this, I would not have you infer that I approve of Nihilism, Communism, or Socialism in their destructive aspects, but I speak of what is to be, of the Spiritual Movement which is now shaking the nations as with the tread of an earthquake. I am not prescient enough to foretell the immediate result that will follow, but I know that all great changes are preceded by anarchy. It is the order of Nature. The present moment calls for great watchfulness. Commons and Lords, Prime Ministers and Kings must be vigilant—no man can sleep at his post. The Royal Crown is no sinecure of ease now. From the Autocrat of Russia to the Queen of England and the Princes of the Commonwealth, a feeling of distrust has taken possession of all rulers. The strong walls of their palaces are not proof against a secret foe. I have no desire to boast, but I am reminded of the fact that I called the attention of the British Government to the critical condition of Ireland.

An ignorant Irish populace is more dangerous and difficult to manage than the ordinarily educated working class of England. A revolution commenced among a squalid body of men, whose very ignorance has caused their subjugation, is likely to be volcanic in its action, as it resembles a Vesuvius in its origin, beginning its fiery disturbance in the lowest strata of life, or beneath the surface.

It was the fish-women of France who organized the Revolution, and stimulated the leaders to their bloody carnival.

The untamed brute, in his frenzy, requires a stronger chain to restrain him than the tamed and educated one, therefore I advised, while yet in office, strong measures to hold the Irish people to their allegiance. They are not sufficiently enlightened to listen to an argument; they feel too intensely the galling position in which they are held, through their own lack of knowledge and the force of circumstances, to be guided by reason and moderation. Their eviction from their households, the distress for rent which overwhelms them, while their tardy crops fail to yield the wherewithal to meet the demands of their landlords, are miseries and sorrows that furnish, indeed, for legislators a study; for the political economist a sad problem; and cause anxiety in the hearts of Royalty, the Houses of Lords and of Commons, and, indeed, throughout all England.

I am no agrarian agitator, and yet I see that the day is not far distant when the immense estates owned by the nobles of England will be more equally divided among the people.

The gods have slumbered long. They will awake and shake the whole earth with their rising. The God of Progress, which is inherent in the common man as well as in the titled Lord; the God of Selfhood, the great I AM which dwells in the humblest peasant's breast as truly as beneath the King's ermine,—that god will awaken and stir the civilized world : he will arise and throw off the chains that have long enslaved him. Night will turn into day, the moon's pale beams give place to the sunbeam, huts and hovels of the poor will be replaced by well-built and well-ventilated dwellings; misery, crime, and ignorance will yield to comfort and education. Superstition will be superceded by knowledge, imparted to mankind by the World of Spirits. BEACONSFIELD.

A CHANGE FROM MATERIALISM.

GEORGE ELIOT.

GEORGE ELIOT, the celebrated Novelist, passed to the Spirit-land some months after Mr. G. H. Lewes.

His communication was given prior to her death. After that event, friends, who had read his communication, enquired how she would reconcile her marriage with his expressions of love and continued interest in her welfare. The Novelist, in her reply, analyses her own contradictory conduct, as clearly as in her Novels she depicts the motives of her Heroines.

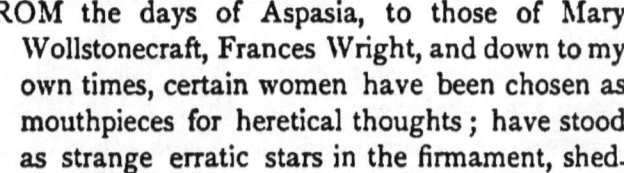ROM the days of Aspasia, to those of Mary Wollstonecraft, Frances Wright, and down to my own times, certain women have been chosen as mouthpieces for heretical thoughts; have stood as strange erratic stars in the firmament, shedding forth a disturbing and independent light, and, at the moment when they had arrived at the height of their glory, and been looked on by their adherents as probable leaders, they have suddenly diverged from the path apparently marked out for them, and left those would-be followers, who had heretofore extolled them as the originators of a new dispensation, to bemoan their loss with despair and mortification.

The peculiar and exceptional nature of woman, at all times more led by her affectional nature than by her love of conquest or ambition for applause, is not sufficiently calculated on by those who hope to use her as a leader.

For years I was looked upon as a semi-leader in the Rationalistic School of Philosophy, a disciple of Spencer, Strauss, and the German Scientists; a materialist in theory; an advocate of strange socialistic views; one who was said to have abrogated the ties of marriage, and to have ignored all religious and social laws, that in any way interfered with the perfect freedom of the individual.

Born with an imaginative and receptive temperament, with an unbounded desire to accumulate knowledge, accident threw me in the society of men of highly developed intellects, of great culture, whose ideas and thoughts, when thrown out, I drank in as a sponge absorbs water. I received their teachings as this Medium receives impressions from the Other World.

From admiration and love, I grew to be a worker with them; and though I apparently accepted the materialistic theory: that at death all conscious thought ceases, (and, from my surroundings and false position, the world accredited me with that belief) yet, stored away in the inmost recesses of my nature, lived another faith—which I myself scarcely recognised—a belief in the Immortality of the Soul;—a belief, I may say it was, a craving, a hankering which I attributed to the superstitious teachings of childhood, that I tried to extinguish,—to crush, as we endeavour to suppress the bad habits of fear and cowardice, acquired in infancy under the training of ignorant nurses.

The chains I had assumed, that seemed so light in the beginning of my career, as I advanced in years oppressed me. I felt their weight but could not break from them.

My misgivings, as to the healthy action of my professed belief, had to be stifled within my own breast. The one to whom I had devoted my life sickened and died. At first I sank into utter darkness. My prop was gone. For a moment it seemed as if the world was slipping from beneath my feet. Moments of anguish supervened. Despair, such as words cannot depict, oppressed me.

Succeeding this, I experienced a sudden revolt of my whole nature. I turned with utter disgust from my long-advocated theories. An inexplicable feeling came over me: I now know that it was the action of Mr. Lewes' spirit that produced this change. It was his sudden awakening into the light of immortality, that caused this magnetic revolution from the theories advocated for years. It seemed to be my own act, but it was an act superinduced by spirit-intelligence.

In the midst of my despair the heavens opened, and I saw him in the Spirit-world, an angel, as witness of the truth of Immortality.

Soon after this a noble and brave man was directed to me, who taught me how to rectify the mistakes of my life; when I was left alone, to be pointed at as an anomaly in creation, he took me by the hand before the whole world.

Putting aside my external wealth, he wedded me for my mental and spiritual gifts. In emulation of his goodness I consented that our marriage should be legalised in a church. If that act was recanting my life-work, and washing out the study of years, then I recanted and washed out all I had acquired by patient reading and reflection.

The dry studies of Rationalistic Philosophy, the bare and flowerless belief that annihilation or absorption ends all with the close of our short earth-life, had seemed to me sometimes, in the silent thought of self-communion, to wear a cold sepulchral aspect. It subdued the warmth and buoyancy of my nature, and made me into a being foreign to my normal self; and I turned with subdued joy to a different social and intellectual career which, thus as I thought, opened to me.

Then arose a curious action in the public mind, which, from censuring me for thinking outside the pale of Christendom, good-naturedly derided me for accepting the faith it had held up for me to follow ! A paradox, indeed !

Conjectures of the public as to my future work, and the truth of the statement made in the heat of my grief that I should write no more, were to be disposed of in an unprecedented manner. I was suddenly called to join my companion who had reached the Land of Reality. He craved the society of his co-worker. The new career on which I had entered was brought, by spirit-power, to a quick termination.

Thus my story of life ended ; its enigma only to be solved in another state of existence. Our heart-yearnings are seldom satisfied on earth. Our ideals fall below the standard of the spiritual image we have created. The soul—thwarted and disappointed on earth, ever reaching out for some higher truth than it can grasp—in the Spirit-world finds its true sphere of action, and rests from the doubts and uncertainties that once beset it.

Mr. Lewes has already given his experience. We each thought to live without the other, but a wise power ordained otherwise. There are some beings who are counterparts. Upon the surface there may be inequalities that cause them to chafe, while their souls assimilate : externally they are unlike ; but, as two streams,—one running over a bare and wild moorland, the other through smiling meadows and bending trees, when meeting together in one great river— they blend into a unit.

So with us: the inharmonies of Life are over,—the harmonies of Immortality have commenced.

SPIRITUALISM:
THE TRUE AND FALSE.

DEAN STANLEY.

IN the city of Paris, on the evening of June 28, the lady through whom these interpretations are given, was entranced, when a few sentences in a low gentle voice were uttered by the spirit Longfellow. The conditions not being favourable, they were discontinued. In a moment the control was assumed by Judge Edmonds, who stated that Prof. Zöllner, Garibaldi, and Dean Stanley were present, and if the amanuensis' mind would concentrate on either of them, such one would proceed. The subject by Dean Stanley having been intimated, it was desired that he should commence; when the following remarks were dictated by him, and transcribed, sentence by sentence, as they came from the lips of the unconscious medium.

IT IS a trite but true saying, that Spiritualism has existed through all ages and in all times. The power of communicating with the departed, when intelligently understood, is one of the noblest gifts given to man, but, when misunderstood, and used for base purposes, it is likely to bring misfortune to humanity.

No one familiar with church history will doubt that apparitions have occurred and revelations been given from time to time. The lives of saints, and of men who have lived secluded lives, are full of testimony to this truth. But, beside apparitions, there have been other signs: voices in the air, raps, and peculiar sounds and disturbances, untraceable to any earthly source, have occurred in certain places and been observed by many parties throughout all the ages before Christ's appearance, and later on, since his crucifixion, even down to the present day.

I have said, that when rightly understood, communion with spirits is beneficial, but when one ceases to think of spirits as spiritual beings, and regards them as material, and low, and lying in their character, they then draw around a mysterious class of beings, who are not spirits but goblins.

These existences are intermediate between men and spirits, and attend such persons as have no desire to rise to high spiritual knowledge; they, not having an exalted purpose, or feeling of reverence, in consulting spirits (such as one should have on approaching any truth), attract these disorderly creations.

Almost all knowledge comes to man through experience, and he has obtained his present degree of civilization and perfection through long ages of experiment, but as his mind has been chiefly directed to investigations of the physical world, instead of excursions into the realms of spirit, therefore, the knowledge he has of those obscure truths is imperfect. Now, it is necessary, in order to understand spiritual laws and the principles governing that world, to devote the same care and patient investigation of them as as has been found indispensable in attaining knowledge concerning the world in which you live.

It is known that your earth is inhabited by an inferior class of intelligences, termed animals. In the Spirit-world there is a corresponding class of beings, who are spirits termed Demons in the old theologies and chronicles of the ancient Hebrews. The term, demon, does not necessarily express bad qualities, but indicates a being between a man and an angel.

I would enter more fully into the character of these entities, if I felt that I could make the subject comprehensible to the reader; however, out of the growth of the spiritual belief a class of students, or explorers, will arise, and by careful examination will discover the laws governing the inter-communication of the two worlds.

Many suppose that all the inhabitants of the spirit spheres have been born on earth, and become refined in the process of ages, so that they have merged into what are termed angels. But this supposition I find to be a mistake: there are spirit essences that cannot claim to have had their origin upon this earth.

Swedenborg's description of Heaven and Hell, I find to be, in the main, correct; though the term, hell, is not an appropriate word for the condition of the undeveloped classes of men, as it would indicate a separate and unprogressive state that does not exist.

The laws necessary for man's development, I discover to be very simple. Many Christian sects teach, that certain arbitrary rules must be conformed to before an individual can enter Heaven, as it is called; but I realized, while on earth, by a close study of early church history, and the customs existing in the days of Christ, that the rules indicated by him and his disciples were very simple, and not at all difficult to be followed.

Man, himself, has become a much more severe taskmaster than the Deity, and from my observation in the spirit spheres, any individual who follows the simple precept of doing good to others, and who lives an harmonious life, will attain heaven and happiness.

In communicating with spiirt intelligences, it will be found, when the purpose is that of greed, and the attainment of knowledge is for base purposes, or for trivial affairs, a class of spirits will respond who prove tricky and boisterous, giving forth foolish utterances, and incapable of imparting ideas or instruction, but able to mislead; of low morals, and entirely devoid of principles. They do a great traffic between the Spirit-world and earth; they are like the money-changers in the Temple, and should be whipped out with a strong cord, as in the days of Jesus.

I would call special attention to such spirits as materialize, ring bells, play on guitars, toss chairs about, talk through trumpets, draw or paint aimless pictures, and amuse themselves and listeners by absurd jargon.

Such manifestations are generally produced by the class to whom I have alluded. They are useful in proving the bare truth of spirit jugglery, but are of no importance for imparting high spiritual truths.

The jugglers of India are assisted by these potent creatures, and the soothsayers recorded of in the Bible obtained their power from the same source.

When men have learned to understand their purpose in the spiritual creation, they will cease to disturb and mislead. Everything should have its true place: the noise and frolic of a holiday are not suitable to the hours of study, nor college recitations to amusements.

Theatrical spectacles are appropriate in time and place; so with spirit phenomena, they should be divided into classes.

Those who desire amusement and to witness spiritual theatricals should seek the materializing mediums; but if the purpose be instruction and serious study, they are to be found among another class of mediums.

It is in vain that intelligent men and women seek the East to gain intelligence on this point, as the class of spirits who produce these phenomena are incapable of imparting intelligent truths.

THE LIBERATOR OF ITALY.

GARIBALDI.

ON the evening of July 2nd, Dean Stanley having concluded his paper at about ten o'clock, the medium was influenced by an ardent, earnest spirit, coming with a gusto truly Italian. It took but a moment to learn that it was no other than the recently departed hero and soldier, Garibaldi. His thoughts were delivered in an impassioned manner, strongly in contrast with the previous eloquent and deliberate Churchman's.

The marked difference in subject and style of delivery within one sitting is worthy of being noted, as both are so at variance with the usual and characteristic manner of the Improvisatrice.

Y BROTHER, you love Liberty! I love you because you are the friend of Liberty! Long be Italia free and united; free to believe, to see, and to think as she is inspired. Free from the oppressors who would keep her in ignorance, in poverty, in hopeless misery.

From Caprera I come to you. I have a spiritual island given to me: it is like my loved home. From here, I look out upon Italy and upon all the world. I have many friends. The soldiers who fought for the freedom of Italy, and died upon the battle fields and in the hospitals, are now with me in this blessed land. They came with streaming banners to welcome me on my arrival. Victor Emanuel, my friend, headed a great troop who came to fetch me to the Spirit-world, where he lived, a few days after the proud magnificent ceremony that was given for me on earth.

Those who say that I was unfaithful, and that I am suffering the torments of hell, are mistaken, and should see me where I am with those who love me, and behold how happy and prosperous I am.

I have loved goodness and truth all my life. I wished to help my beautiful Italy to rise from the dust, and to aid in restoring her to her ancient glory. My motives were comprehended by the beings in the Spiritual World, and I was rewarded on earth by the love of my countrymen, and now, in the world into which destiny has placed me, I am rewarded in a three-fold manner; for I can still watch over Italy, and I now have the society of my former comrades, of my child, of my early companion, of Victor Emanuel, and Mazzini. I have spoken to Pius IX. God bless him! A good man, but not very far-seeing.

THE LAW OF CREATION.

CHARLES DARWIN.

THE spirit of this great man made many efforts to convey his ideas through the Medium. He filled her mind with sublime thoughts which she could not convey by language. She saw, as in a mirror, the earth in its first stage of development. The air seemed heated, like fire, filled with flying monsters, the earth torn by convulsions, monkeys and satyr-like men swarmed before her eyes.

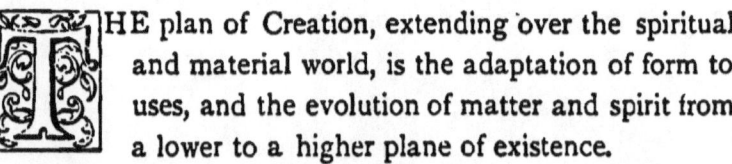HE plan of Creation, extending over the spiritual and material world, is the adaptation of form to uses, and the evolution of matter and spirit from a lower to a higher plane of existence.

In the early geological periods, only the grossest forms of life could exist, or contend with the crude elements and disturbed state of earth and atmosphere. Thousands and thousands of years elapsed ere man appeared upon earth, not then the perfect Adam, but a being a little higher than the animals, and "lower than the angels." A creature resembling the wild savage: there, first, we find the spiritual nature shooting out, a phosphorescent-like emanation, living a semi-sentient life between two worlds, the spiritual and material. When separated from the body, this fine net-work of impalpable spiritual existence becomes compact, and a solid body in the atmosphere of the Spirit-world, even as certain gases that are invisible to the eye, become, under peculiar circumstances, solid and ponderous bodies.

The soul, being like man, a progressive development of every created sentient form, is admirably adapted for navigation through space. Analogous to light is its power to penetrate space, and in the rapidity of its motion, it speeds, like a bird seeking its nest, to its immortal home. This, if its spiritual instincts are developed; if not, guided by its *love* and *will*, it hovers over its useless body, or the former place of its habitation. To its surprise it finds itself with a form adapted to diving into the depths of the sea, of ascending into the air, of penetrating matter, and traversing the earth; almost unlimited in its powers, but dependent upon its intellectual development and the expansion of its moral faculties for an intelligent use of its new organism.

I have been accused of endeavouring to prove that the monkey was my grandfather or progenitor. Critics might as well assert that I had stated an ant-hill and Chimborazo were one and the same. I find an analogy between the two; so between men and animals there is a strong likeness: they are the outgrowth of the same Creative Principle. The monkey stretches out his long arm, and gathers the fruit from the tree-top for his food; man, with a shorter arm and more creative brain, invents means to gather the fruit and food necessary for his sustenance. Mentally he stretches out his arm and reaches the Infinite. His soul is ever putting out invisible antennæ, which proves analogously that there is a spiritual sphere for these "feelers" to reach, as, by a law of creation, when certain organs become useless they cease to exist. The fish inhabiting the lowest depths of the ocean are found to be without eyes, as sight is not necessary in their dark submarine abodes.

Man having a spiritual nature, which is constantly reaching out into the invisible world, must find ultimately what it seeks. The page of natural history will teach the investigator, that a lower form must finally ultimate into a higher one. Where are the antediluvian animals that trod the earth ere it reached its present state of perfection?—the mastodon and flying dragon, the monsters of every variety, that filled the earth and air during the different geological periods?

The more man's wants increase, the more his power to gratify them increases. As he rises in the scale of creation, he is constantly changing his position, and adapting himself to new conditions: from the wigwam, the hut, the tent, of his ancestors, he has developed the artistic palace of the present day.

When this world ceases to be useful to him, he rises to another, better adapted to his growth. When he becomes too ethereal to exist upon the planet earth, he rises to a more spiritual one.

Astronomers will tell you of planets known to the eye of science, where a bird's feather, so light as to elude your grasp on earth, will there fall like a dead weight to the ground; and where the mite in the sunbeam, to you invisible, will there appear upon a large and grand scale. The invisible, formless atom, subjected to the magnifying lens, is found to possess a shape of wondrous mechanism, and to move, instinct with life.

The student of nature, who doubts the existence of Spirit because he cannot see it, has but to recall these facts. The spiritual mechanism of his nature is not yet entirely demonstrable by scientific experiments, but if research into the occult phenomena of Spiritualism be continued, the desired proof will surely come. If I could have lived a hundred years longer, I should have been able to demonstrate the evolution of an angel from a man, as readily as I could prove the evolution of the man of science of to-day, from ignorant and cannibalistic aborigines.

NICE, MARITIME ALPS, *February* 28, 1883.

DESTINY.

MARY, QUEEN OF SCOTS.

AMID the orange groves of Nice, the lovely spirit of Mary, Queen of Scots, visited the medium. Her influence was very gentle, casting a soft glow over the spirit of the Sensitive.

IN LIFE I was attended by an evil spirit, who presided over my birth, and followed me to the scaffold.

In youth I might have chosen a good guide, but I succumbed to the evil spirit of my destiny. I was saved from being entirely lost, by a long imprisonment, and by my final execution; otherwise one more lost spirit might have been added to the multitude who wander up and down the earth, seeking whom they may devour, delighting in evil, in discord, ruin, and crime.

Happily I am not of them. Years of penitence on earth, as a spirit, has saved me from such a career. I am the favoured guide of a few whose lives I influence for the benefit of humanity. My pilgrimage on earth is pursued by their side. I suffer when they suffer, and rejoice when they rejoice.

Three hundred years ago, I lived upon the earth. It seems to me but as a day since I became a bride! The human soul is capable of encompassing a vast experience. The man of eighty years looks back upon his childhood's days as a living present. Thus the spirit contemplates three or four hundred years as a tale that is told,—Time is a whiff, a puff of smoke. *Yesterday, to-day*, and *to-morrow* comprise centuries of time! The Past, Present, and Future is all there is of time and eternity.

I possessed the gift of attracting individuals; fortunate, indeed, is the person who has this gift, and uses it for the benefit of his followers, like Christ, Socrates, Confucius, and the hundreds of the world's saviours, who have existed since the beginning. Such persons are a power in the Spirit-world, for evil or good; they draw within their orbit their satellites.

Evil and good spirits fill the air, even as animalculæ cover the vegetable world,—invisible, destroying or sustaining. People who have appeared evil on earth, often are not wicked, and in the Spirit-world are seen as they are,—circumstances, which threw a black cloud over their life, being dissipated by the light of truth. Others, who were considered as saints on earth, now, like myself, walk unknown and unhappy, the attendant of some persecuted medium, or some bright lady's shadow. You pass many a queen, and person of rank by earth-birth, unconsciously, among your humble acquaintances, and often brush past their spirit-garments in your disdainful moods.

Evil is more powerful, psychologically, than good. Any man with will-power can draw evil spirits around him to accomplish his wishes. If he will aggrandize himself and trample down what stands in his way, fearless of good or God, he will find assistance, and become a Nero or Napoleon. Only the fluctuations of his own will can defeat the efforts of his evil guides.

So, a woman may become, like myself, a Mary, Queen of Scots, and, syren-like, lure men to their destruction, or as Mrs. Fry or Mother Anne, devise means for the amelioration of the unhappy condition of a portion of the human family.

I am asked, if numbers possess a mystical significance? I reply that certain numbers are representative; that the magical figures used by the Asiatic race, are recognised by the ancient Hindoo, Arabian, and Chaldaic spirits, and by them employed as signs, conveying predictions of events involving the destiny of nations.

I want this book to succeed, to be read ; all the energies of my being I devote to the Spiritual Cause.

Let those whose life, like mine, has been presided over by an evil genius, be thankful when they can expiate on earth the crimes of their life, and thus break the psychological tie which would bind to an evil destiny.

John Knox, who was a clairvoyant and medium, warned me against the evil spirits that attended me, but his manner was harsh, and I was blind. I could not believe him, more than thousands of people now believe the prophecies of mediums. Luther, Calvin, Knox, Melancthon, Wesley, and Swedenborg, were all mediums, inspired and chosen to prepare the way for the reception of spiritual truths. Andrew Jackson Davis opened the path to the Revelations of to-day. People are daily becoming more and more receptive to light from the Spirit-world, and to believe the fact given centuries ago, that myriads of spirits walk the earth, good and bad. "Mene, mene, tekel, upharsin."

NICE, MARITIME ALPS, *March 1st*, 1883.

FOR FRANCE AND FREEDOM!

GAMBETTA.

WITHIN a few days after the interment of Gambetta's mortal remains, upon the castellated hill overlooking the blue Mediterranean and the City of Nice, the Medium visited the spot, made beautiful and sacred by a towering pyramid of floral souvenirs, tendered by delegations from every section of France.

The atmosphere was clear and balmy, while the neighbouring snow-clad mountains seemed to image cathedrals of whitest marble in the sky, and the sad murmuring of the blue sea below, a funeral dirge to the immortal spirit of Léon Gambetta.

These conditions were exceedingly favourable for the reception of Gambetta's influence by the Medium, and upon returning to our hotel this communication was received.

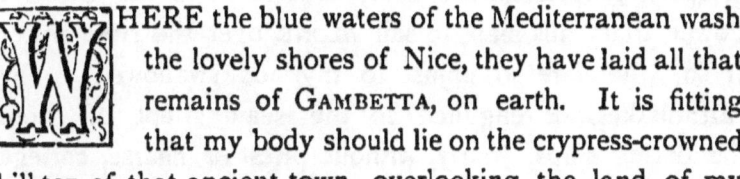HERE the blue waters of the Mediterranean wash the lovely shores of Nice, they have laid all that remains of GAMBETTA, on earth. It is fitting that my body should lie on the crypress-crowned hill-top of that ancient town, overlooking the land of my birth, and the Republic of France, that I have loved so tenderly.

The flowers of my native land, gathered by willing hands and wet by loving tears, sent to decorate my grave from every city, town and hamlet of France, have raised for me a monument of affection, surpassing in beauty the sculptured mausoleums erected to Emperors and Kings.

No priests followed my funeral cortege, with white robes, donned to cover the lies they were living: lies to nature and manhood. No chanting boys, vociferating words they comprehended not; no false candles flickered their paganish eyes upon my corse; no church pageant ushered my body back to mother Earth; but, in place, a whole nation, lovers of " Liberté, Egalité, et Fraternité," arose and followed, on a long journey, the remains to its interment, of one who had led them reckless of his own life, to break the chains of superstition that had held them in bondage.

Foreigners may cavil at the manner of my burial. Priests rail over it, "Légitimisté" bemoan France for her weakness in permitting the heart of the nation to throb according to its natural wont.

Who, let me ask, instituted the rites over the dead, customary in Catholic and Protestant countries? Did Christ or Mary, Jehovah or the Holy Ghost? Did the Creative Power, that calls man to sail ALONE over the river Styx? If so, wherefore so unjust to myriads swallowed up by earthquakes, or engulfed in the sea: swept off from foundering ships, yearly, without priest or hearse, cortege or ceremony?

Who ordered priests for the burial of the dead: Are they nature's addenda to that event? Truly, No!

There is one man, though a priest, whom I would gladly have seen at the grand national fete of my burial. I embrace him,—he is called Père Hyacinthe. Vile men scoff at him, Catholics deride him, some Protestants shun him; but the angels recognise him! And I render him my thanks for the gift he laid upon my tomb, for the fearless words he spoke in my behalf, for the fraternal feeling with which he stretched forth his Christian hand, and placed a cross of immortelles upon my unhallowed grave.

O, listen to me, ye people who bow down to forms! I tell you, many a priest, who scoffs at Gambetta, leads a life a hundred-fold more damning than he did; and when the cowl is torn from off them, in the World of Spirits, they will appear guilty before him whom now they curse.

I do not claim that every act of my life was without blame, but I do say, I did not profess one creed and live another: I did not preach a morality that my own life belied.

Shame on ye, my countrymen, who revile Père Hyacinthe for his honourable life. He has said of me that I was religious. What he has said of me is the truth: I was religious. My Christianity was that of Christ's: a friend of harlots and sinners. I worshipped a God as truly as the most pious monk or sincere believer. My God was *Truth*, and I confided in my God. In whom do the Christian nations confide? In priests and traditions!

Would you roll back the wheel of time, turn the earth back on its axis to the days of Paganism, repeat the deeds of the multitude when Paganism was tottering on its feet, and a new religion (that of yours to-day) was about to supersede the old one? Socrates was given poison to drink by the religious demagogues of his day, because he spoke against the worship of Venus and Bacchus, Jupiter, and the Lares and Penates of the household; even as I have spoken against the priestly rites that you hold so sacred! What has civilization gained in intelligence for two or three thousand years, if it would force a man to be buried in accordance with certain dogmas? If human affection is to be repressed, and a nation like France to be anathematized for not enforcing the mummeries of Paganism, and for following my body to the grave in accordance with the laws of Reason and Justice, I inquire—Where is your vaunted Christianity? Are ye truly followers of the meek and lowly Jesus, who was laid in his sepulchre without rite of church or sanction of priest?

Oh! if priests would but know how useless their forms are to usher a man into the World of Spirits, they would quickly drop their crucifix and candle, their beads and censers, and let loving hearts lay poor humanity in the grave, even as they have placed the infidel GAMBETTA.

Down, I say, with a priestcraft which holds men in ignorance and poverty. People must be educated, that their future life in the World of Spirits depends upon the life they live on earth; that prayers to saints, virgin, or prophet cannot assist them on earth or benefit them in heaven, unless followed by noble deeds and virtuous life.

As to my state in the World of Spirits, no masses said by priests, nor paid for with a king's ransom, could have placed me in a better position here, than the one I now occupy from my own acts, inclinations, and desires. My thoughts turn ever towards France! I live again in the councils of the Republic. Unseen I attend the debates. I endeavour to influence the party to which I belonged, to extend knowledge to all.

Let the People be taught that the Next World is a real world; that oppression and tyranny produce misery in both worlds; that a fiat has gone forth from the World of Spirits to the nations of the earth, that Kings and Queens, Emperors and Popes, shall no longer coin gold out of the ignorance and misery of the multitude, for knowledge shall cover the earth. The reign of Superstition is past. People no longer believe that an individual's condition in Heaven depends upon his manner of burial. Let Religion and King-craft cease to be a trade, a business, and the multitude will soon learn how to live and die in accordance with Nature and God's design.

THE MUSIC OF THE FUTURE.

WAGNER.

RICHARD WAGNER's communication is remarkable as demonstrating, to interested parties, the electrical current that pervades the universe, conveying thoughts from the Spirit-world to individuals, and telegraphing ideas from one person to another. The Publisher of this Work wrote to the Medium at Paris, August 2nd, 1883, thus: "I have been thinking of Wagner and his life aims, and the future music; and I would like an article from the late Emperor of Russia." Strange to say, the Medium had received from both these parties their respective communications two days previous.

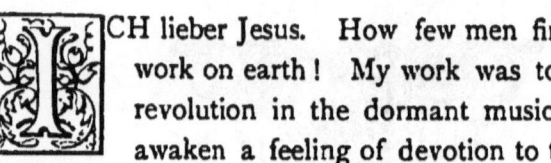CH lieber Jesus. How few men finish their life-work on earth! My work was to inaugurate a revolution in the dormant musical world, and awaken a feeling of devotion to that highest of spiritual gifts. The music that I have left behind is to be the Music of the Future. It is but a great fragment; a Sphinx head. After ages will produce the genius who will complete what I have left unfinished. To him will be given the power to hear voices from the Spirit-spheres, as I did, telling him to press on and overcome all difficulties, till he reveal the wonders of the Spirit-sphere of Music.

Mark the rhapsodies of the musician: he is called a madman. He shakes his head from side to side, his hands tremble, his whole being vibrates to the silent melodies, the harmonies that strike his ear from an unseen universe; he is swayed by invisible influences: controlled like David, when he played on the harp and sang before Saul, and drove away the evil spirit by his sweet notes.

The trivialities of life crowd too closely upon the artist, for him to listen as he should do to the voices that come to him from the Soul of the Universe;—from the forest, from the stream, the mountain, and the fertile plain,—pleading with him to forget personalities, and render the songs of Nature, with the feeling divinity has impressed upon them. Hark! Bend thine ear to the wild music of the wind; hear how, from the faintest wail, it rises in crescendo till it thrills thee with very agony! Canst thou see the source from whence it cometh? Does the representation of Æolus, holding the winds in his hand, add to the majesty of that awful sound? It speaks to thee of the black forest of pines, through which is has travelled; of the giant trees it has snapped in twain; of the mountains, bleak and bare, down whose icy ravines it has hurled the adventurous traveller. It speaks of the sea, with its waves dashing mountain high, hissing about the doomed ship, whose mighty hull it tosses like an egg-shell—up into the spray-laden sky, and down into the abyss of waters—with its human freight of awestricken souls, gasping their final farewell to wife and children, home and earth, in one bitter cry of despair? What artist can render this sublime diapason of Nature?

In the Music of the Future the individual will be out of

sight : the long, slender hand of the musican, gleaming with gems, will not be seen to distract the senses of the audience from the combination of glorious sounds. In the great future, personalities will merge into one grand *whole:* as the noble Cathedral does not speak of the patient carving, the minute grinding of each workman, but addresses the spectator as a great completeness, a blending of various thoughts and labours into one sublime work.

It is the stars collective, that make the wonder of the heavens. Nature is communal. Be like Nature. The Community is the truest representation of Heaven, each working for the good of the whole. What discord we make when we scream louder than our fellows! but a sustained pitch : ah! that is glorious. If you rise to a high altitude, draw all up to you; teach them the way by which you ascended the heights,—spire rising above spire, peak above peak, all in one grand unit,—like the Alpine range of mountains, the lesser adding to the greater. That is true life, art life, musical life, eternal life.

Music is the language of the Gods. It is worship. Would you unlock the mysteries of Future Life? Music is the key.

In the future whole communities will think, breathe, and speak music. As men strive for gold, now, will they strive to attain musical perfection. Let me sing of my Fatherland. The nearest point to spiritual life on earth is the musical community of my Fatherland : Where the whole town's life is centred on music ; where the children lisp in harmonious numbers; where the recreation of the day and the labour of the day is music; where the king is as simple as the citizen, and to develop the divine capabilities of music, that master art, sacrifices the etiquette of court life, the leisure and indulgence contingent on his position; and with the interest of a true king and father of his country, devotes his wealth to the harmonious development of his people.

Music is a life-work, not an hour's recreation. In the future there will be musical centres, where all lovers of music will congregate; where the wealth of the nation, instead of being expended on useless pageants, will be used in furnishing music for the people. A life of Arcadian happiness will follow, and earth become a counterpart of spiritual spheres.

The simplest air you can sing brings you *en rapport* with Spirit-life. Every musician and composer is a medium. The moment a person raises his voice in song, he is lifted into a spirit-atmosphere.

Music has been diverted from her legitimate sphere, and made to warble weak love-ditties, like its sister art, Painting, prostituted to an ignoble end; when it should express the heroic exploits of each nation, and the aspirations of the people; revive from the dark ages the strains in which blind Homer chanted his Iliad to the listening Greeks. Let music sing to you of the struggles of a great Nation for Freedom. The operas of the future will be historic records, revelations of the innermost heart of humanity; not the hurried work of one evening, but days and weeks will be gladly given in listening to these dramas of the world's history, that the Music of the Future will reveal.

Then press on, my musical students, in your noble work. A great revival in every sphere of art awaits the world.

The fabled golden age is about to dawn. The cycles of eternity will roll back to view. The magnetic centres of the Spirit-world are reached. That vast source of inspiration is open to mankind. America, the youngest power on earth, sprang direct from spirit spheres, and has become the pioneer of the older nations. She has taught us how to talk with the mighty dead, the unending universe of spirits.

The people of my Fatherland follow in her footsteps. Spiritualism is spreading over Germany, and mediums from all parts of the world will hasten to my country to hear the *Music of the Future*, that spirit musicians will perform in the art-centres of Germany and Bavaria.

OUTRE MER! OUTRE TERRE!
BEYOND THE SEA! BEYOND THE EARTH!

LONGFELLOW.

The beloved Poet of America essayed to write a poem, similar in rhythm to "Hiawatha," through the Medium, depicting in it his departure for, and entrance into, Spirit-life. But the verse seemed combined with other influences than his, and Longfellow, at the request of friends, re-wrote it in the form in which it now appears.

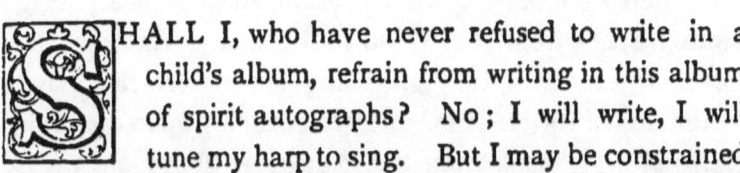HALL I, who have never refused to write in a child's album, refrain from writing in this album of spirit autographs? No; I will write, I will tune my harp to sing. But I may be constrained to sing my old songs over again, to invoke the muse of bygone days. May not a musician rejoice in his own music? Wagner's soul responded to the strains of the "Niebelungen Liede" and "Parsifal," as sympathetically as if he had not himself composed them : for all true poetry and music is an inspiration, and we poets but re-echo the chimes struck in Spirit Spheres.

I should like, as the bards of old, to wander from hearthstone to hearthstone, and chant the Lyrics and Epics of Spirit-life. Through what strange scenes have I passed, since I left my dear old home on earth. Shall I tell you with what indefinable awe I awaited the signal from CHARON, who was to ferry me across the dark river? Many whom I had loved had sailed away with him long years before. Wife and friend he had borne from me; my locks had become whitened by age while waiting for his coming. Would my loved ones recognise me in the Better Land, now that I had grown old and grey? True, as I sat alone in the deepening twilight, often "The forms of the departed entered at the open door; the beloved ones, the true-heared, came to visit me once more." I felt their shadowy presence, but an intangible something divided us. I longed to meet them face to face, as in days of yore.

The summons had come. I was going to them. Suddenly I became insensible to earth and its surroundings. I had entered the dark icy tunnel, *death*, that forms a passage through space from your world to the next. As some lost traveller, wandering through falling snow over the glacial mountains of Switzerland, emerges suddenly upon the sunny plains of Italy, so I, from the blackness about me, rushed out into a magnetic stream of light, through which, in some incomprehensible manner, I floated, as we appear to float through the air in our nightly dreams. A lethargy, that had for a few seconds enthralled my senses, passed off, and I found myself looking out upon a lovely landscape. A vast park stretched before me, covered with a moss-like verdure, ornamented with ethereal trees, whose myriads of small leaves, agitated by the magnetic air, broke like the spray of a fountain against the sky.

As I moved on through the air, towers and spires, minarets and buildings, resembling those of earth, passed before my eyes, while here and there rose great cathedral-like structures of a pale, rosy, semi-transparent substance, looking not unlike palaces of ice, glowing in the rays of the setting sun. I was fearful that what I saw might prove to be phantasmagoria,—a beautiful mirage, that would fade away; but it was real: it was a beatified earth, even as a spirit is a glorified human being.

Then crowded upon my memory, as white-faced billows break over the sea, recollections of all my friends, who had passed from earth during the years of my sojourn there. This was accompanied by an unutterable longing to see my dear wife and companion of early years. While in this reverie, there broke upon the air a sound like rushing water, like children's joyous laughter. Nearer and nearer it came, resolving into a flood of music. It was as if the melody of Rossini and Bellini, with the majestic strains of Handel and Mozart, were united in one grand symphony.

This overture subsiding, a grand chorus of voices arose, singing words familiar to my ear; words which, as they have touched the heart of the great public, prove the divine sympathies of the human heart, and the link that joins man to immortality; for these were the words they sang:—

> "Life is real, life is earnest,
> And the grave is not its goal;
> Dust thou art, to dust returneth,
> Was not spoken of the soul."

To hear, in the clear spirit air, these prophetic words of

my muse, sung to the music of the heavenly spheres, filled my soul with ineffable joy.

Then gathered about me my friends; they were all there, —people whom I had seen borne to the grave in years past; friends of youth and manhood clustered about me. We spoke together. They congratulated me on my arrival in the Better Land. In sweet converse they led me to a "city of gold," a city lit by unearthly light, neither of the sun nor of the moon, for the God of Love giveth it light. In that Home of the Soul, an effulgence magnetic rises from loving and true hearts, that dwell there; from myriads of benevolent souls, who illume the dark places of earth, and guide the ever-seeking, upward-reaching Spirit of Man into a state of HARMONY and LOVE!

A TRIBUTE TO THOMAS CARLYLE.

JANE CARLYLE.

THE Medium had been ill in Paris, two or three chilly spring days, and was lying on her pillow in a despondent mood; when a peculiar, quick voice spoke to her: "You must get up, and find paper and pencil; then you can go back to your couch, and I will write something for you."

So urgently was the Spirit's demand reiterated again and again, that the Medium was forced to comply. That eager spirit proved to be Mrs. Carlyle, and in this curious manner the public has been favoured with her communication.

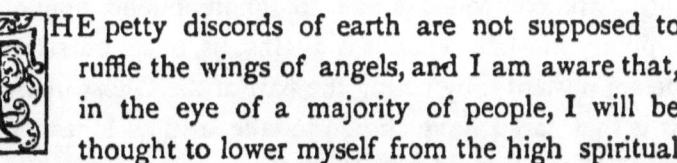HE petty discords of earth are not supposed to ruffle the wings of angels, and I am aware that, in the eye of a majority of people, I will be thought to lower myself from the high spiritual estate to which I have ascended, through the sceptre of King Death, by taking part in the controversy now existing concerning Carlyle's peculiarities, and his neglectful treatment of his wife (myself). But I shall endeavour to set History aright, by giving my posthumous testimony as to the unrecorded goodness and tenderness of the great Giant.

What a levelling age this is to live in and to die in! A man is not safe even when he gets to Heaven. People delight in throwing down the idol they have been worshipping, and the same voice that acclaims it a god, the next moment denounces it as a thing of straw, a soulless nonentity. In their fervour to prove that they are too keen-sighted to be duped, and in their efforts to obtain an equilibrium of the scales of Justice, they lean too heavily on the opposite side, and throw more dust and mud into the scales than necessary.

Folk believe that every wrong is righted in the Spirit-world, and that we, its angel-denizens, have only to fold our fair wings, while the great Judge places all our enemies on His left side, and finally sends them to add fuel to the flames of Hell.

Unfortunately, or fortunately—according to your morals,—this belief, like many another fable, has no basis in reality, for we, who have left *terra firma*, and soared into Angelland, are compelled either to ignore public opinion, like ordinary mortals, when it is against us, or set ourselves right before posterity, by acting the part of the Ghost in Hamlet! It is that part I have chosen to take, and as I have only a woman's weapon wherewith to combat, I begin, as my sex usually does, by *asserting*. Therefore, accordingly, I assert that THOMAS CARLYLE was ever thoughtful of my comfort and happiness. The external man appeared cold and obtuse sometimes, but the soul was gentle and remorseful. His great body did not always harmonize with the action of his spirit. Like the ponderous hulk of some ship, so mighty in its own weight, it cannot respond immediately to the rudder; but when it does move, it is the stir of a giant. So with Carlyle: his friendship for me increased with years; death did not diminish it.

He was a medium for the Spirit-world. Through him they poured down truths upon the earth, which will never cease to benefit mankind. He was opposed to shams and self-deception, and in seeking to avoid these evils, he conducted himself in a manner which the public has interpreted as cold and selfish. Too much of an anatomist for his own earthly good, he analyzed his feelings so closely that he not only permitted himself no cloak to cover a deformity, but actually made a deformity appear where it was not, from overzeal.

In the Spirit-world his clear, searching intellect, his warm heart and truth-loving soul, place him in a sphere high above his cavillers. I am happy to say that he is with wise, good, and exalted spirits, for the judgments of heaven are not as the judgments of earth. Appearances deceive on earth. A polite, suave manner, though it hide a false heart, and is mere dross, will pass for pure gold, while the brusque air and rude demeanour, which covers a loving heart, is cast aside as worthless. Carlyle was above and beyond his detractors.

I am disturbed by the publication of all these letters, which are not like a true mirror of the soul, but resemble a green and unequal piece of glass, which distorts the image presented. Affairs that take place on earth affect the Spirit-world, just as events transpiring in England affect America, and *vice versa*. It is an old saying, that history cannot err, and that time, which cools the heated opinions of men, brings right judgment to the public mind at last.

Carlyle desires to be judged without favour. Take a knife and dissect him as you will; but does that dissection, however thoroughly it searches the body, discover the soul? The inner emotions of a man, which are his true self, are never definable. They cannot be written upon paper or spoken. His best thoughts could only be read through clairvoyance. His spoken judgments were often harsh, but his thoughts were kind.

How like vultures men rush upon the fallen prey! If Carlyle were still upon earth, would his life have been written and commented upon as it has been? Why does the public keep old garments, that a man has outgrown, and insist that they are his true measure? Let any man read a letter, penned by himself ten or fifteen years ago, and he will fail to recognise his own authorship. How little of our best thoughts we can put into a letter, and how much foreign to our true feeling creeps in!

Earthly views and criticisms are flashed across the spirit wires soon as published. Carlyle and I have a lovely mountain home. Sitting near him ofttimes, or flying by his side over the purple mountains, I commune with him about things of earth; about this Book of his Life, which has created such a talk. I do wish the Medium had read it, but she has not done so. I told him I would seek a medium, known to all the literary spirits, of whom I had heard D'Israeli and Macaulay speak, and through her I would proclaim how good he had been to me, and how mistaken people were in judging from the external.

Carlyle's judgments were harsh, because he read the

motives of men clairvoyantly, and saw often that they were not actuated by the high principle they professed. He did not want to be thought a hero; his life was a disappointment, because people expected him to become a leader, a teacher, whereas he only expressed thoughts that came to him inspirationally : thoughts he felt strongly, but which were given, as all true teaching from the World of Spirits is given, to be accepted or rejected according to the plane of development, and not to be forced upon the hearer with threats of annihilation to those who differed.

Emerson, the American, and Hawthorne, and Parker, Longfellow, Darwin, Stanley, and Coleridge, visit us from time to time. Then we have an intellectual feast. If it is not "Table Talk" it is "Bower Talk," for we sit under the vines and trees of Heaven, and speak about Heaven and its inhabitants : of the mighty wonders that surround us, and of earth and its people. We have very curious trees here, quite different from those of earth, covered with numerous small transparent leaves, some of a golden red colour, others of a pale silverish hue, which give out light like a subdued sunlight, and an odour like roses and pines. Then we have singing trees, like the trees of fairy lore, whose leaves, as they open and close to the magnetic air, send out a few sweet notes, not unlike a bird's trill.

Carlyle has quite regained his youth, and is actively busy studying the lives and spiritual development of the great teachers of earth; of Christ, and those who preceded him.

He tells me that he felt my loss, after he realized that I was actually gone from him, most acutely, and that I seemed to be in the room with him almost constantly; that my personality never became lost, or a myth to him. The truth is, that I was with him: I used to feel his heart ache, as a part of myself, in the Spirit-world.

I am happy to have this opportunity to talk about him, and to praise him to those who love his works; to the few who really take the trouble to think and analyze a man's character. He was impatient of human nature, because men, who are really Gods, dwarf themselves into pigmies.

Who could sympathize with his restless, aspiring soul, craving converse with Olympus' Jove himself? Mediumistic spirits like his are never understood on earth : they scoff at the weighty matters that affect the generality of mankind. The influence of the Spirit Spheres is over them, though they know it not. They have a prescience of their eternal home, and chafe under the ills of time ; like as the caged eagle, snuffing the air of his cloud-capped eyrie, beats against the bars of his prison, in vain efforts to reach his long-lost home !

SPIRITUAL APHORISMS.

BENJAMIN FRANKLIN.

Mr. Burns, the Publisher, wrote from England to the Medium, residing in Paris, asking if she could induce the spirit of Benjamin Franklin, who had introduced Modern Spiritualism to the world, to inform the public why so many mediums were detected in fraud, and why such good mediums as the Davenport Brothers had degenerated into exhibitors of the phenomena, at the same time renouncing the truths they had once fostered. Franklin appeared—a genial, whole-souled spirit,—but would only answer his questions by the following aphorisms, in which we hope the riddle will be expounded to the reader.

IT is a well-known axiom, that fraud engenders fraud.

The psychic force of a *determined doubter* calls up lying spirits.

Go to a spirit-circle, determined to catch the medium at fraud, and at that very seance the most reliable medium will act like the "devil."

Have the faith Christ had, and spirits will materialize in your pulpits and reading-desks. Doubt them, and they will throw bells and tambourines at you, and say the mediums did it.

———

The whole Arcana of Nature, spiritual and material, can be opened by the man who seeks, with patient investigation, to penetrate its mysteries.

———

Spiritual knowledge, like gems hidden in the bowels of the earth, is only to be reached by patient upturning of the soil.

———

Do not attempt a spiritual friendship with spirits who would degrade you morally or spiritually. A man is known by the company he selects, and mediums who fraternize with the spirits of Arabian mountebanks and Egyptian jugglers, should be received as exhibiting amusing phenomena, which will demonstrate spiritual truths, only as a trickish monkey demonstrates the origin of man.

———

The spirit who shouts your name through a trumpet, and greets you familiarly, may tickle your vanity, but cannot convey to your mind grand thoughts, or prepare you for nobler life in the Spirit Spheres.

———

Spirits are the souls of humanity. Among them are charlatans, beggars, murderers, thieves, simpletons, mingled with good and pure souls: intelligent, loyal, honest, and sympathetic beings.

Do not be discouraged when you find your pet medium to be a *fraud:* there have been false prophets in all ages of the world.

"Fret not thyself because of evil doers," has been the prayer of aspirants after spiritual truths, from time immemorial.

No man can navigate the air in a child's boat. To navigate the spiritual heavens requires also the appliances of science.

Franklin's kite and key unlocked the electric vaults of heaven, started the Rochester knockings, revealed the electric telegraph and telephone, and will discover the secrets of Life, Death, and Immortality.

It has taken a hundred years to develop the electric telegraph. Give us a hundred years to develop our spirit mediums.

The spirit who takes off the medium's coat, while his hands are tied behind him, is likely to be a Chinese or Hindoo juggler, who, though he perform a feat of legerdemain, should not be received as a guide in spiritual or moral affairs.

The great statesmen and thinkers, who have passed from earth, do not entertain themselves by performing curious tricks to amuse and awaken the wonder of mankind.

Into the Spirit-world are poured daily hordes of wild spirits from Asia, Africa, and Europe: the fanatics of India, the savages of the forest, the murderers, drunkards, and half-idiots that swarm the earth. Receive each according to his degree, and do not form a spiritual friendship with those who would tempt you to drink, swear, or act untruthfully.

———

Accept pure and noble teachings, though they come from an ignoble source, as the thirsty traveller drinks fresh, pure water from a dirty cup. Remember that a golden vessel may contain rank poison.

———

Truths never change though they may assume a new garment, and the manifestation of them alter. The imperfect likeness, fastened by Daguerre on a sensitive plate, foreshadowed the accurate portrait of to-day.

———

Crude experiments only prove the possibilities of future developments. Had you a lens powerful enough, you could see your face repeated billions of miles in space. So are truths repeated and handed down through the long ages from Spirit Spheres. So in spiritual science, the ugly, distorted image produced to-day will be superseded by the clear photograph in the future.

———

You cannot force the heavens, by a storm of artillery, to hearken to your prayers. Speak to Nature in her own language, and she will listen to you.

Hashesh and opium-eating produce a low form of spiritual trance, and introduce the unfortunate indulger into the degraded dens of spiritual society.

It may be optional with you whether you communicate with spirits by means ot a medium or not, but it is a law of life that they should attend and influence you. On your own actions and culture depend the class of spirits who attend you.

By shutting your eyes you cannot prevent the sunlight from warming you, neither by denouncing Spiritualism can you prevent spirits from influencing you.

He who will only be fed by fairy tales in spiritual matters, will find the "Spirit-Bride,"—who treats him to a curl of her golden locks, and spins out fine meshes of lace before his wondering eyes, drawing out of space yard after yard of the cobweb texture,—is only a human syren with mask and wig, "a counterfeit presentment" of some spirit Aspasia.

Praise John, a schoolboy, for turning out his toes, and all the boys will imitate John, and cry—"We turn out our toes, too." Praise a spirit for talking through a trumpet, playing on a banjo, or showing a ghostly face through a cabinet window, and the mediums who assisted at the seance will feel—"I can do that, too"; and will, the next time, imitate the reality.

Go to hear a famous opera-singer, and you will return home humming the air, and think the tones of your voice sound quite like the prima donna's. A medium discovers within himself a power of reading names written upon paper pellets, heaped together promiscuously. That gift attracts a wondering crowd; straightway his vanity is roused, and he feels: I did that wonderful thing myself, no spirits about it. Next time, he decoys a paper and reads the name himself, then confesses! *Exit.*

In the Christian Church it is said of a man, once a member, who degenerates, that " He has *fallen from grace.*" How many a poor medium *falls from grace.* Unable to withstand the flattery of the world, he simulates the great gifts that at first were genuine, and becoming a *fraud* in the eyes of the public, ends as a *sham*, failing to distinguish the false from the real.

A man who would go wrong under the noble teachings of *Spiritualism*, would have gone wrong, as Judas, under the pure teachings of *Christ.*

If we extol Christ's example because he was a God, how much more should we admire it as he was a *man.*

All the possibilities of Heaven and Hell are incarnate in man, as the octave embodies the grandest musical compositions for a full orchestra.

PRE-HISTORIC AGE.

EGYPT.

THE following communication was given by spirits of a pre-historic period. In the year 1880, the Medium, while visiting the romantic country surrounding Lake George, made famous during the American Revolution, was entranced in one of the pine forests, which surround the lovely lake. The control desired her to visit Egypt, that thus she might get in perfect rapport with the spirits of that ancient nation. She visited Europe in 1882 according to their direction, but was unable to travel as far as Egypt, which soon became involved in war with England. The communication is unfinished.

I AM the Morning Sun. Before the Pyramids were formed, I existed. Centuries have I been ranging through the fields of eternal space. The thoughts of the Great Invisible can only be gathered from the mountain-top or the desert plain. In

the mind of the Seer, dwelling in the midst of a great city, thoughts are gathered from men, not from the eternal plane; not from the great Master Architect.

To know truth as it existed in the past, we must seek for it in Egypt and in India: in the vast solitude of the tower-reaching mountains of India, or on the boundless plains of pyramid-crowned Egypt.

The spirits that converse with men to-day come from the cramped cities, confined houses, or petty palaces of modern times; but the spirits that existed before the so-called Christian era, will lead you up to a broader space, and will unfold to you a panorama that shall be a counterpart of the higher heavens.

Visit Thebes. View the ruins of the mighty temple that was there raised to the creative power of the Unseen. Contrast it with the cathedrals and diminutive churches that Christendom of to-day raises wherein to incarcerate their own idea of their Deity and their Jehovah.

The soul of the worshipper, in the days of the centuries past, when I trod the earth, worshipped the Unseen Principle, with its sublimest powers. Not as to-day, with cramped mind, imbued with thoughts of inferior deities, offering up a moiety of its attributes to the Invisible.

In ancient days, the soul that had passed from material life to a spiritual one, could return and re-incarnate itself in some other form of humanity, thus gaining in wisdom through the experience of many lives.

For ages the Egyptian dynasties have been swept from sight by the crude, physical nations, which, in the order of nature, have sprung up on the globe, and for centuries have been fighting their way to what is termed civilization.

Now, the state of volcanic eruption, as I may term it, has subsided. Egypt, with her Sphinx, with her Pyramids, rises on our sight; again to be re-incarnated after the lapse of these mighty cycles of time, and to reveal the mysteries of an Unseen World, which has so long been hidden from mortal vision.

This mighty, revolving current, that has swept around humanity, will carry you onward until you will behold literally the temples of the Great Unknown, and have spiritually entered the mysterious Pyramid, that leads to the Upper Spheres.

THE FOLLY OF HERO-WORSHIP.

THOMAS CARLYLE.

AUGUST 28. Judge Edmonds having expressed his regret and disappointment at the delay in the publication of the book, he was followed by the spirit of Carlyle, who gave the following communication, remarking when finished, that we must put the odds and ends together and make what we could of it. The point he aimed at, was to show that things are just as unreal in earth-life as we suppose them to be in Spirit-life, and that we on earth are actually living a spirit-life. Carlyle did not appear satisfied with his communication, and gave the second part with great rapidity and earnestness.

THE world expects a literary man to make a good appearance. He must be carved after some fashion they have in their minds, and if they discover him in some ordinary mood or house-dress, they are disgusted, and he suddenly falls in their estimation as an author of genius.

Since my autobiography has shown me to the public in the character of a homely Scotchman, with all the attributes of my native soil bristling about me, they have ceased to regard me as one of the wonders of the nineteenth century; and now, if I still further remove my wrappings, and appear as a ghost visiting from the grave, I fear that I will lose my prestige entirely, and the name of Carlyle will be lost to future generations.

Alas! that humanity should prefer the unreal to the real, and demand that a man should wrap himself in the theatrical garment of a statue, rather than that he appear in his natural guise!

This tendency to hero-worship, and of making an unreal image of some notable character, is a relic of barbarism, and should not appertain to the civilization of the nineteenth century.

The ancient Assyrians represented their heroes by the bodies of lions with eagle's wings. The British Museum is filled with these monstrosities, that belong to neither heaven, hell, nor earth.

This same monstrous way of deifying men has been followed in describing Heaven; and the heroic idea of heaven, the general heaven that is pictured by the so-called Christian, is about as near to the real heaven as a carved crocodile's body, with the head of a bird, is to that of the Egyptian Kings of antiquity.

The greatest traits of Christ's character, supposing him to have been a God, were his human traits.

Christians try to magnify him into some impossible being; so the world would have idealized me, if I had not lifted the curtain and let them see within my cabin windows. So of Dickens. People perused his tales, and imagined some ideal man as the author of them. After reading the record of his life, they ceased to read his books. He was the same man, his books were the same. And so when one returns from the Spirit-world, many would say, "He would not talk in that strain," because his remarks do not answer to the imaginary man that they have created.

I am vexed and mortified at the *claver* about me and my doings, that my "stepping out" has given rise to; though, according to the illogical conceptions of spirit that are held by the majority of people, my veins should run milk and water or an "airy nothing"; and I should witness this literary war about me without more feeling than an idol of stone. But I have laid aside my woollen mittens, and no longer sit over a fire nursing my bloodless body, as in my latter days: I have revived, and risen out of the "Valley of Dry Bones," and feel all that is said and thought about me. I have grown communicative, almost garrulous. I must tell the world what I have been doing; so it will believe it is my *ghaist* which croons so loudly.

I have seen and conversed with Frederick the Great; with Voltaire and Rousseau; with Napoleon the First; with the blood-thirsty Robespierre; with Marat and the leaders of the first French Revolution; with Richter, Goethe, and Schiller; with Byron, Coleridge, and Shelley. I have even seen the *wraiths* of Socrates, Plato, and Christ.

I was not in harmony with the age in which I lived; its trivialities vexed my soul. I belonged to the past. Schiller and Goethe were my bosom friends. I was like a meteoric stone, flung on earth by an electrical tempest: out of place, and having no grounding soil where I was; gazed upon with wonder, and not comprehended by the people around me.

There are a few such individuals upon earth, whose lives are counterparts of a phenomenon that occurs in the physical world, for they are like strange shells and sea-weed from a tropical sea, that are washed up on a northern coast,— lone types by themselves, out of consonance with their surroundings.

The harmonies I sought for on earth, I find in Spiritland. If I had comprehended mediumship, I might have been a more contented man, and have understood the cause of my unrest. I was a medium and knew it not. My first work, "The History of the French Revolution," on which I had laboured, and which was destroyed by fire, as I then thought by an untoward destiny, was rewritten by the aid of spirits, and was the means that first brought me *en rapport* with invisible influences, and caused me to give to the public a work of far greater power than the first one, whose loss I bemoaned.

I grew to live with the mighty thinkers of Germany, France and England. They held converse in my presence, and aroused my mental and spiritual faculties to their utmost capacity.

What a race of spiritual Titans might inhabit the British Isles, if her immortal sons would give up their fox-hunting, and acceptance of soul and body-grinding creeds, and investigate the laws that govern Spirit-life! The tramp of myriad invisible spirit feet is causing her social fabric to tremble; it rocks to and fro. The cries for help—from her thoughtful artizans, from the silent tillers of her soil, the blackened and poison-breathing miners in the bowels of the earth—reverberate through the Angel-spheres!

Cohorts of spirits, from Russia, Germany, France, and Italy, have banded together to aid the struggling and famishing crowds, of what are called the "lower classes," into a position of independence. Not only in England and Ireland is this spiritual movement in progress, but throughout the whole mortal globe. In China and Japan, Russia, France, Germany and Italy, the sound of the supernal tocsin is heard. Can it be stamped out by the power of kingly heels? Who can forge the chains to hold the man whom spirit power has released from a dungeon? The battle is not only against Earth but Heaven; against Powers of the air, and invisible armies clothed in the panoply of spirit hosts : Where, O thoughtless Emperors, Kings, Lords, and Squires! is the weapon that will smite them down?

O rugged Scotland! home of my boyhood: the spirit of thy Highlanders and Lowlanders; thy love of freedom; the poverty of thy soil; thy mountains sparsely clothed with elements to grow food, have saved thee from the rapacity of the rich and noble. Thy Kirk-bells have rung out their harsh theology, without breaking the spirit of Hope dominent in thy people. Thou hast cherished the gifts of "SECOND SIGHT," and thus kept up a perpetual summer of communication with the inhabitants of the Next World.

Now open thy arms to receive the new Christ of the nineteenth century—SPIRITUALISM!

THE CAUSE AND TREATMENT OF CRIME.

JAMES T. BRADY.

A FRIEND of Mr. Brady having met the Medium in France, where she was sojourning, requested that a communication be given from him for this book. The request was complied with, but as the Medium was taken ill about the time the meeting was to take place, the friend was obliged to leave the city, and the communication was given to her alone, before entirely recovering her health. Subsequently, on the gentleman's return to Paris, the article was submitted to him for perusal. He stated that he did not think it sufficiently characteristic of Brady to warrant its publication, and he thought it must have been mixed with other influences, which was the case, as Mr. Brady was obliged to request Judge Edmonds and others to assist him in controlling the Medium. It is thought best by the Editor to present it to the public, to judge of its merits and resemblance to its accredited author.

HAVE been impelled by the desires of a friend who read law under my instructions, to add my testimony to that already given as to the real life in the Next World, and to demonstrate by my communication that spirits do not lose their individuality, or the learning which marks them on earth.

Many who knew me will ask: "What can James T.

Brady have to say for himself?" Others will exclaim: "We remember him, he was a great criminal lawyer, and the friend of a wretched lot of rogues!" That is true. I had to defend many a man accused of breaking the law; besides, I was acquainted with all the prominent New Yorkers of ten or twelve years ago, and I must confess that they were a rather "roguish set." I have followed up their lives from the time I left the earth to the present day, and have helped many a one out of trouble. Obscure and intricate cases always had a fascination for me. Crime is just as much a study to me now as it was on earth. Though ignorance and poverty produce social disorders, yet a natural proclivity to evil deeds is the cause of many a dreadful act.

I was blessed with a large social and sympathetic nature, and through that was led to help my fellow-men when in trouble. Judges and lawyers are accused of taking bribes, when their sympathies are aroused and they endeavour to save a man from the gallows. Let us err on the side of mercy. A human judge should image his great prototype, the Almighty Judge of all; but a judge like old Judge Jeffreys, of England, appears to be the type of judge that many persons desire, who believe in *punishment* not *reformation*.

During all my long experience in courts of justice, I found that the man we punished was often *not* as culpable as the man we let go free. I recall the sensation created in the Spirit-world by the entrance of Wm. M. Tweed, whose terrible punishment and miserable ending, after a short but brilliant career of defrauding his Government, should prove to men that retribution follows evil-doing. He suffered more than many who were accessory to his guilt, for human justice is a one-sided affair, and those persons whose tool he was escaped visible punishment; but if their inner lives could be read, it would be seen that they are daily being punished, for violation of law, human and divine, brings with it pain. He was not an intrinsically fast man, but he glossed over his conscience, as too many men do, by telling himself that he would benefit mankind out of the wealth he should acquire, by defrauding others and betraying his trust.

Men, who go astray from principles they know to be right, are like ships driven out of their course by tempests: they do *not* obey their rudder, and are forced by adverse winds and cross seas, one influence after another, upon the rocks, and are shipwrecked at last.

A man called to public office, has often associates thrust upon him, whose magnetic, psychological influence upon him is bad.

Evil-minded and unprogressed spirits are drawn to the clique. People are seldom aware of how much they are influenced secretly by their associates. The subtle acting of one mind upon another, is a truth which can only be comprehended by students of spiritual science. Men are like sheep; where one goes the other follows, even if it lead them to perdition.

Individuals generally have the power of self-psychology, and for the purposes of gain can make themselves believe that wrong *is right*, though their inner spirit-self tells them the truth; and that is called *conscience*.

Events that occurred in New York immediately after, and a few years previous to, my passing away, presented themselves to my memory vividly as I conversed with this Medium in Paris, drawn thither by the friend of whom I have spoken. I revert to the career of Fisk and Stokes, to Judge Burnard's troubles, to the Wall Street gamblers, to the fearful struggle for riches going on in high places, the low criminals and weak men clamouring for justice.

You must remodel your law code if you would mete out justice to all, and sweep out your law courts, and the trial-by-jury system must be revised. I never found twelve unprejudiced men yet, who were capable of deciding an important case. A jury will often convict a shiftless, penniless fellow, on account of his appearance, but let a man of position—a minister, clergyman—come up for trial, and though he has seduced a girl, and murdered her to hide his sin, they will let him go scot free!

The treatment of criminals by the State and society, is altogether wrong. It is not based upon principles of wisdom or justice. The Government should *not* coin money out of criminal labour. Punishment should be educational, and the surplus funds accumulated from the earnings of criminals, should be applied for their benefit, and distributed to them as incentives for good behaviour, in the form of soil, land, farming implements, mechanical tools, clothing, food, or money, according to their necessities and ability to make use of the advantages offered.

The beneficial effect upon society, caused by modifying the laws of capital punishment, can be seen by reverting to the page of England's history, when men were hung for stealing, a hundred years since. A poor fellow in those days, wasting away with scurvy on ship-board, would be hung as an "abandoned fellow," if he stole so much as a potatoe to keep off the dread disease; he was considered beyond all help in this world or the next. Observe how, from a nucleus of such outcast wretches, sprang into existence those prosperous English colonies of Australia, that are at this day the wonder of the world, and the homes of thousands of as good men as those who have never escaped from a court of justice.

Give the worst man a chance, and he may become a saint, and place a good man in bad surroundings, and he will probably become a sinner. Spiritualism, with its teachings of progression, has been sent from the angel-spheres to enlighten men as to the falseness of the doctrines of total depravity, and inspire them with a desire to reform from the animal into the intelligent spiritual plane, so that their existence in the Spirit-world may be one of use and pleasure instead of pain and disorder.

I only wish poor, misguided men, who anathematize their fellow-creatures, and picture the torments that divine wrath will bring upon their sinful heads in another world, would divest themselves of these baneful ideas, and investigate the laws of progressive development, that they may prepare themselves and their disciples for the enjoyment of the Spirit-world as it really is.

The only way to be happy on earth or in the Spirit-world, is to cease wishing to bring your fellow-men or enemies to justice. The poor man loves to indulge the idea that there will be some amend made to him in the Spirit-world for his poverty on earth, and that the rich man when he gets there will be worse off than Lazarus; that is a sweet morsel he delights to chew in his poverty. Do you think such an idea could help him on in heaven? No! it would drag him down to a condition worse than hell, and many are in that condition, I regret to say. To enjoy heaven you must give up being judge, one man of the other; each individual must do the best he can, irrespective of what others do; then he can live contented in Paradise.

And yet to produce order in society, it is necessary to make laws and enforce them. Place upright judges in office, like Judge Edmonds, and do not force them to *resign* because they are *Spiritualists*, and the good effect of their treatment of criminals will be felt throughout the whole social status.

It is a futile policy to execute men, and send them into the next world, thinking thus to rid the earth of them; for they return with redoubled vigour, if ignorant, to have their revenge, and influence their boon companions on earth to commit increased outrages against society. England thinks to quell the Irish spirit of rebellion by extermination. She bribed an informer, and sent a dozen *men* into the Spirit-world upon his information, supposing in that way she could eradicate the *Invincibles;* but, as in the classic fable of the "Dragon's Teeth," she will find that a thousand armed spirits spring up, to disturb her, from the seed thus sown.

What you cut down on earth, rises with redoubled vigour there. If the world could only read history aright, it would perceive that crime is contagious, and that one wicked murder is always succeeded by others more horrible, because evil is not eradicated by death, or execution upon the gallows.

We have no prisons in the Spirit-world, but we have educational, reformatory localities and colleges; but the two worlds are so intimately interblended, that we cannot produce a radical change in bad men, until the world commences her reformatory process. The prisons of earth are relics of the dark ages and the days of Inquisition; they have not kept pace with the advance of civilization. While the public schools of America are her crown of honour, her prisons are her disgrace.

EDUCATIONAL INSTITUTIONS IN THE SPIRIT-WORLD.

PETER COOPER.
Founder of "Cooper's Institute," New York City.

PETER COOPER, one of the benefactors of New York, lived to pass his ninetieth year in the full possession of his faculties. He, in spirit, visited the Medium in Paris, as she was walking in the gardens of the Trocadéro, and expressed pleasure at seeing through her the handsome Grecian buildings which, he said, were not unlike some of the temples of learning in the Spirit-world. He surrounded the medium with an aura of tranquil, benign happiness.

AM safely over, but what a strange world I have entered, widely different from any preconceptions I had formed of it, although I was somewhat familiar with Spiritualism and its teachings.

I see life everywhere about me: busy, happy life. Spirits flying to and fro on missions of love or mercy; many have a light like a sun radiating from their head and figure. One can see these lights at a great distance; shining in various colours and different degrees of magnitude, they resemble the glory depicted by ancient painters around the Virgin and Christ. When moving toward you, and within a mile or two of where you are, the light appears to open, and you recognise in it some friend dear to you, or some individual known to you by engraving or photographic likeness, approaching to talk with you, for though it is not necessary to be near to friends to speak with them, yet spirits generally desire to be in close proximity with those they love. The telephone has been known and in use from time immemorial in the Spirit-world. The means of conveying thought among cultivated and highly developed spirits is by a mental process. Thought generates electricity, which, like lightning, conveys the idea, and photographs it on another receptive mind.

Every invention on earth that has benefitted mankind, appears to have sprung from this Spirit-world. I remember to have read, years ago, in "*Strange Visitors*," of a visit to Henry Clay's home, and of how he communicated with distant parts of his building by means of electric cords. That was the foreshadowing of an invention since developed on earth, which will assist in making mankind all one harmonious family.

The electrically-propelled car, by which Irving glided over the spirit roads, will shortly be familiar to all the inhabitants of earth; they will traverse the globe as we traverse the fields of space.

I am astonished to find the number of temples of learning that exist here. I have been shewn some one-hundred times as large as the Institute I established after my humble fashion on earth. They are circular in form, or shaped like a magnet, with an outer corridor to different entrances, and an inner court, with fountains throwing up delicious essences and of invigorating perfume, while trees and strange flowering plants embellish the parks by which they are surrounded. Trees, here, are unlike earthly trees, the leaves being of variegated colours, resembling the autumnal foliage of the American forest.

When I speak of temples of learning, I do not mean mere schools for the study of arithmetic, geography, writing, &c., that appertain to the earth-plane. These Spirit-colleges are intended to develop the soul of man, and teach him his relations to mankind; to instruct him in the wonders of the sidereal heavens, impart to him knowledge of the inhabitants of the sun, moon, and stars, the numerous worlds in space occupied by various tribes of men. To aid him, also, in experimenting in chemistry and sciences, by which he can explore the uttermost extent of the universe; to instruct him in political economy and laws governing humanity, that he may develop means to ameliorate the condition of the unprogressive and helpless portion of mankind.

From these grand Spirit-universities are promulgated all the progressive doctrines that startle Christendom. All scholars and clergymen who secede from the doctrines taught by the Churches, are in spirit-communion with the leaders of these Spirit-institutions.

It was from this superior source that Shelley received his inspiration, and wrote under spirit-dictation his "*Queen Mab.*" which, at the age of nineteen or twenty, caused his expulsion from an English college, and brought about a new era of thought. Here Theodore Parker received the light which illumined his works. Here the science of communicating with earth was first developed. From this quarter

Darwin, Wallace, Varley, Crookes, Tyndall, received the ideas which have made their names famous.

From my earth-efforts to give free instruction to the youth of America, in engraving, painting, designing, and kindred arts, I have been chosen for similar work in the Spirit-world. I find enough to do here. Enormous numbers of youths arrive daily in the Spirit-spheres. Many are ignorant of all arts and sciences, and have had no opportunity to develop their mental and spiritual natures. I have formed a school to teach them how to educate their inventive and constructive talents, for the power to construct and build is God-like. The most unhappy spirits are those who are idle, and know not what to do with life; who have no idea of employing the time in useful labours.

Old age is a blessing. Experience brings wisdom. I am thankful I lived as long as I did on earth. I have now commenced to grow younger, but it is the youth of a full-grown tree, renewing its leaves and sap with the spring.

SPIRITUALISM, A LIBERATOR.

ROBERT BRUCE.
Ancient King of Scotland.

A FRIEND was asked to suggest some names from whom it would be useful to receive communications for this volume. That of ROBERT BRUCE was given amongst others, and the following message was received in response.

I HAVE come from a far-off world. I belong to the dim past. I was called BRUCE, *King of Scotland*.

I am of another people than those who exist at the present day. I lived in a semi-barbarous age, among a warlike race of men, believing in the supremacy of kings by divine right. Yet I was a lover of liberty, and was chosen then by the Spirit-world to inspire a never-quenchable desire for freedom in the hearts of the Scottish people.

Five centuries have come and gone since I led my little band at Bannockburn, and again since the advent of Spiritualism in this Nineteenth Century, I have been chosen by an invisible hierarchy as a leader for England and Scotland, to impress the Church- and Kirk-bound people with the truths of Spirit-communion.

One man I have elected as my battle-axe, that is James Burns: he possesses the fearlessness and persistency of the ancient Scots, who when they saw a truth were not afraid to acknowledge it. Slow to change, but once convinced of an error, no considerations of policy would prevent them from adopting the right.

I feel a kinship with America—I claim brotherhood with her people, for as she resisted the tyranny of the old English rulers, so I, and my followers resisted the encroachments of that mighty kingdom; and so will Spiritualism resist her oppressors, and form a mighty, independent organization or body, that will draw under her banner the whole human family.

It is not only for to-day, but for all time. It cannot be trodden out. No edicts of kings nor courts of law have power to suppress it; no church maledictions nor priestly denunciations will hush the spirit of *Truth* which is in it.

It is supported by invisible powers: sustained by hosts from a superior world; *not* demons, but intelligent, God-loving, good-living, purified, sanctified souls (according to ecclesiastical parlance).

As the great American leader, George Washington, laboured until he saw America had become an independent nation, feared by her opponents, a refuge for the oppressed, a defender of man's spiritual and physical rights, an advocate and supporter of progressive development,—so I, following his noble example, will labour on earth for the Cause of Spiritualism, both in England and Scotland, until it becomes a recognised power, and is received by the Church and its denouncers as an equal and friend, of whom they will seek knowledge; a faith in whose loving protection they will find defence from the *superstitions* of the Past and the *doubts* of the Present. What is to be done now, is for Spiritualists to stand by the Cause they have espoused.

THE AUTOCRAT'S DOOM.

CZAR OF RUSSIA.

ANOTHER name suggested was that of the late Czar of Russia, ALEXANDER II., whose experience forms a contrast to that of the foregoing.

BELIEVED in Spirits. If I had followed the advice given me by them, I would have been living on earth to-day. My position and political influence prevented me from following their teachings. I would not listen to the warnings that they gave me. I found it necessary to keep the people down by strong means. I believed it indispensable, and I banished many of my subjects to the desolate regions of Siberia, while my own conscience told me that I was doing wrong. Spirit voices warned me, but I resisted their appeals, for I was hemmed in by circumstances, by courtiers, and customs, and the tyrannical usages of my predecessors. But fate does not listen to such weak excuses. Justice cannot heed them. The progressive development of mind has uttered the cry of—" Down with tyranny."

I heeded it not. My punishment was swift and sure; and did not end with my immediate taking-off. Even now, when I enter the earth sphere, I experience the dreadful physical sensations I passed through at the terrible moment of the explosion; my head feels like a pent-up volcano.

I have been obliged to pass many days in the cold climate of Siberia, in desolate regions in the Spirit-world, forced by my own conscience to visit those wilds, and endure some portion of the misery I have inflicted on others.

I see from my standpoint in the Spirit-world, the masses of Russia in a state of fierce agitation, though hidden from view, similar to the condition of the elements in the bowels of the earth, when the low rumbling is heard that portends the coming earthquake.

I little thought on that eventful morning, while riding in my coach, inspired with feelings of pride in my powerful army, with their acclamations ringing in my ears, that the people whom I held in such strong chains and subjugation, were in a state of revolt; and were about to hurl me from my throne, by the subtle dynamite, into the boundaries of the Spirit-world.

I wonder not now, that men should be traitors to their Sovereign. I wonder not now, that the assassin should silently plot against the nobility; for deadly dynamite is not more cruel than the tyrants of Russia have been to her people.

At length my successor has been crowned Czar of Russia; and may he be more worthy of his position than I proved to be. If he listen to the cries of his people for justice, then the volcano over which he stands will not break. If he refuse to listen to the warning voice, he will be removed, as I was, suddenly and violently from life.

Adieu, adieu! I will return again. I here feel a rest while holding your hand.

CAPITAL PUNISHMENT CONDEMNED.

LORD FREDERICK CAVENDISH.

ANOTHER political contrast is afforded by the short but pregnant message of the estimable Nobleman who was assassinated in Phœnix Park, Dublin. The lesson to be derived from the testimonies of these Rulers should not be forgotten by all who occupy responsible positions in the government of nations.

THE English Government has revenged my murder, but it does not help me, in thus sending these hot-headed Irish Invincibles after me into the Spirit-world. They will do more damage to the Government here than they could have done had they been permitted to live, and been imprisoned or banished for life. I must say it is a great mistake of the Government.

What with Carey and all the brood, we will have enough of "Mother Carey's chickens" to betoken a storm, for according to the sailors' parlance they are the forerunners! I cannot well see my way out of the difficulty, but I know this, that as long as people are executed and sent into the Next World, trouble and discord will reign on earth.

It will have to be given up, this killing one man because he killed another. As for Ireland, she will have to wash out in tears of blood her secret plotting against innocent persons. I had intended to help her. My wife has nobly set forth her views and mine on the subject, when I was cruelly attacked and butchered. "O the bloody taking off!" as Hamlet says. I should like to call the attention of Her Majesty the Queen, and of the noble Lords of Parliament, to the unrighteousness of bribing men to betray their fellow-murderers to death!

We instinctively despise an informer, and yet the law officially gives a premium to a criminal for betraying his fellow-criminals. It is a shocking precedent to evil-doers.

PARIS, *July 20th*, 1883.

SPIRITUAL STATE OF GERMANY.

KARL FRIEDRICH ZÖLLNER.

Professor Zöllner gave his communication with difficulty. A foreign country, and perhaps foreign language, interfered with the perfect flow of his ideas.

I WAS on the eve of unravelling mysteries that have baffled the scrutiny of every scientific eye. I expected to decipher the problem of life. The inscrutable was within my grasp, when the Power, that presides over these veiled mysteries, swept me from earth !

I hastened with alacrity to the Next World, because I thought, with the acumen I had acquired, I could operate in the World of Spirits, and force my College professors and students, who laughed at me and doubted my experiments, to stand aghast at the convincing acts I would work against their materialistic philosophy. But I find myself under a different set of laws from those that governed me on earth ; subject to a seemingly involuntary action, which propels me from one point in space to another, as the heart propels the blood through the veins.

Impelled by this force, I have followed the Medium to the New World of America, and hope to reach, by my words in this book, where I have failed to make myself visible.

The German mind is said to be tinged with mysticism. Our legends point to good and bad influences, to powers in the air guiding our actions. The people of my Fatherland are mediumistic; they comprehend the doctrine of affinities. They feel when danger is nigh, they thrill with a mysterious influence when an enemy approaches. Many of our sensitives can tell what is being done in a house miles from where they are. The writings of Gœthe symbolize our spiritual state.

Side by side with our perceptions of intangible influences, has grown up a spirit of scepticism. Our failure to demonstrate what our instincts perceive, has resulted in a materialistic school of philosophers, who demand sensuous proof of the immaterial. That proof is vouchsafed to-day. I have given to the world my experiments.

Let any candid investigator place himself in connection with space, by means of a medium, and he will find a tangible proof of invisible power. A cold hand will perhaps touch him, when no earthly hand is near; or he will hear sounds in the air, strange raps, which will answer intelligently his questions. I do not assert that every person can invoke these phenomena, for there are peculiar persons whom I term *intermediates*, who are endowed with the power of communicating with the dead; but in every family there can be found one, so it is for all to search as I did.

Like all Materialists, I had a hankering desire to believe in a future state. I wished to have the existence of intelligence outside of the physical world proved. I discovered that space was pervaded by an intelligent force; to that I gave the name of "a new dimension in space."

The Delphic Oracles are hushed, but the power that once animated them roams through supersensuous air. The Magician has passed from the civilized world, but the cabalistic figures that unlocked his secrets are within the reach of every student of nature.

Scepticism appears to know no middle path. Scientific Professors, instead of candidly examining the claims of Spiritualism, assume the hypothesis that life does not exist, if not cognizant to the senses under conditions which exclude spirit-manifestations.

The learned world has long doubted the existence of the ancient city of Troy, asserting that it was but a Homeric legend, a myth created by a Poet. To-day their lengthy arguments, disproving the existence of such a city in antiquity, have been thrown to the winds by the researches and discoveries of the learned and intuitive Doctor Schliemann.

A like fate will follow the false arguments of the Materialists, for the discoveries of the present day have unearthed the NEXT WORLD.

ASTRONOMICAL ORIGIN OF SPIRITUAL PHENOMENA.

CROMWELL FLEETWOOD VARLEY.

This communication was given incognito, and only through urgent demand was the name appended.

S I am told that this book is not written for the purpose of establishing a creed, but to reveal individual experience and opinion of life in the Spirit-world, I will give my views thereof. From observations I have made during the short time I have dwelt in the Spirit Spheres, I will state that I have discovered that there are several magnetic belts encircling the earth, similar in general appearance to the belts that surround the planet Jupiter.

These are inhabited by the worst class of spirits who pass from earth daily and hourly, by earth-bound spirits, and by those who are held by ties of affection to friends on earth.

Beyond these zones, I have been informed by exalted

spirits, there exists outside of the earth's spirit-sphere a vast Spirit World, traversing the innermost heart of space like a comet, emitting a vaporous spirit-light, like the nebulous trail of a comet. This grand Spirit-world pursues its course through trackless space, making its circuit and reappearing in the earth's atmosphere every two thousand or eighteen hundred years.

When its sublimated magnetic strata touch the earth, disturbances both spiritual and physical occur. The planetary system becomes agitated by the vicinage of this strange magnetic orb. The earth quakes and trembles, the sea recedes from its bounds. Volcanic mountains pour forth fire and smoke and melted lava, while whole districts of the earth are swallowed up by the sea, and new islands are formed.

Earth grows spiritually excited, and ghosts become visible, from the projection of the spiritual magnetic aura into the earth's atmosphere. The human mind becomes disturbed by these influences, and commences to explore anew the mysterious Realm of Spirit. Theological disputes and discussions, as to the soul's power of prolonged existence after the decay of the visible body, become rife.

Preternatural sounds are heard, strange agitations occur in the human frame, and a feeling of doubt and suspense prevails over humanity. A general feeling of breaking up, of some stupendous disrupture, occurs. Revolutions and wars break forth, from the disturbed spiritual condition. The vague perception of spiritual harmonies, that the proximity of this sublimated world produces, gives rise to dissatisfaction with the prevailing order of human life.

A desire to obtain a more balanced relation between the physical and spiritual condition of man, results in disorder and unrest.

One thousand eight hundred years ago, when this Spirit-comet reached earth in its periodic flight, Christ, the great medium or mediator, as he is called—the meaning is the same,—was born. The radiant star seen in the East by the wise men was the magnetic light thrown out by this spirit sphere. Jesus, feeling and knowing the vicinity of this spirit aura, predicted a new heaven and a new earth. Spirits met him on the mountain heights, and walked with him in the solitary olive-groves. He became one with them. He prophecied, he raised the dead. Perceiving that the rites in the Temple, instituted to spiritualize the people, had become a dead letter, a mere matter of form; and that the people were perishing for heart-food and soul-bread; and that the sacrifice of bulls, rams, and goats to the Spirit-God did not reach unto the heavens, but had become a cloak to hide gluttony and evil-doings, and that the observance of Church laws was more enforced than kindly deeds or soul-full actions,—he commenced his spiritual teachings. Strange phenomena occurred in his presence. The earth was disturbed at his crucifixion. After visiting "purgatory," one of the spiritual belts encircling the earth, he ascended into the celestial heaven or grand cometary system, that was at that time still within the earth's view.

Thirty or forty years is the time that this heavenly visitant remains contingent to earth.

In the present century the Spirit-comet has appeared, and

has been accompanied with decided advance in spiritual science. Instead of in the East, in America has the influence of this great spirit-body been felt. The secrets of the Egyptian Soothsayer have become universally known through Mesmer, and the number of "Intermediates" has increased in proportion. The trail of the Spirit-comet is passing out of the earth's atmosphere. Marvellous spirit inventions have been developed on earth, projected from the Spirit-world during the last thirty years, which is the time required for this enormous nebula to pass through the earth's atmosphere. As it recedes, it agitates the air with its vanishing wave, but soon it will enter the fields of eternal space, and mankind will wonder what has become of their ghostly visitants!

The spiritual phenomena will gradually subside, but like the receding wave of the ocean they will have placed the race on a higher plane than it occupied before. A new Religion will take the place of old Theology, and the final development of men into gods, knowing good from evil, and the encompassing of the whole earth with knowledge, as the sea covers the sands of the ocean's bed, will result. I say the phenomena will subside, but the spirit guardians and house spirits also, dwelling in the belts surrounding the earth, will remain here to protect and educate the spiritual nature of man.

Besides this periodical incursion of spiritual beings from the Spirit-comet world, there occurs the more frequent inroad of lesser spirits from the belt that spans the globe. Those spirits are in a state of progressive development and change, and join the vast army in the higher sphere when they have gone through a necessary earth experience. They are made up of the general mass of mankind, who daily pass from earth in the order of nature.

A perception of the inter-relation of the Spirit-world with earth, has existed since man's life on the planet began, but as the generality of mankind were occupied in exploits of warfare or in cutting down the wilderness and founding of empires and kingdoms, a few individuals were set apart as priests to investigate the spiritual phenomena. A class of persons, whom my friend Zöllner terms "intermediates" or mediums, revealed the mandates from the invisible world to those whose physical condition prevented them from receiving the information direct. Discovering that by fasting and concentrating their minds on certain forms, they could receive this inspiration, the learned formed a clique to hold these mysteries from the common people, and retired into seclusion so as to enhance their knowledge, and guard it thus from becoming common property.

Nearly eighteen hundred years previous to Christ's advent, in the golden days of the Egyptian, Grecian, and Jewish period of maturity, the same phenomena occurred, during the visit of this Spirit-comet. Spirits walked and talked and partook of food on the earth visibly. The Oracles were active. Prophets and sibyls abounded, and the spiritual influx upon the earth resulted, as it ever does, in humanity taking one leap in advance in civilization.

Tribes and nations, that had lived as the wild beasts, became spiritualized. Arts and sciences flourished. Inventions were born, discoveries made, and a new religion was founded. Men ceased to worship crocodiles and bulls, and adored an invisible, protecting Deity.

So, back through time, can be traced the action of this periodical spirit visitor, elevating mankind by the influence of its aura, and by the proximity of progressed spirits. So, also, in the future, centuries from to-day, from nineteen hundred, will this winged Spirit-world return from its mission to other earth's, and for a period of years hover over the globe, disseminating light and spirituality.

MISTAKEN POLICY OF THE CHURCH.

J. W. COLENSO.

WE hope the reader will be as much pleased with the Bishop of Natal's communication as we were in receiving it. It is modest and yet soul-reaching. It was given to the Medium while residing in Paris, France, in the summer of 1883, at the time of Cetewayo's defeat. It was supposed the Bishop would allude to the disaster of his friend, the Zulu King, but he did not.

THERE are so many grievous wrongs that need righting on earth, that a man who is interested in his fellow-beings cannot live contented in Spirit-life unless he is aiding the good work of reformation.

It is a great mistake of people to think that the old way is the only right one, and to go over the old rotten bridge because their forefathers went over it. Most men will follow a beaten path though it take them miles out of the way; but I say, blessed be the fearless pioneer, who strikes out a new, shorter, and better road to the same point!

Now, in England, the Clergy, whom I duly respect, have got into the habit of running in a rut, and it is difficult to make them take any other course. Why should we arrogate to ourselves that our way is the only way to Heaven? I call the attention of my clerical brothers to the unchristian-like condition of a community, that necessitates the passage of a promulgation called "The Burial Act." Look at the dreadful scenes occurring in many parishes, where the Clergyman refuses to permit a burial, in the Churchyard, of one who differs from him in mere religious forms!

You call the Zulus barbarous, but they are not as barbarous as these falsely-called "men of God," *Christian* priests.

This is the very spirit of bigotry, that lighted the fires of the stake! that tortured the martyrs of the early Church, and crucified *Jesus of Nazareth*.

The Spirit-world is disturbed by such monstrous deeds, committed in the name of Christ. It is time for us dead priests to awake, and shake our dry bones.

Look at the tenacity with which the Church clings to the old translation of the Bible, tinctured as it is with the prevailing ideas of the old translators. Call your common sense to your aid, and ask if now in your day, you could not make a more faithful translation: if the mind, free from superstition and bigotry, and educated in technical knowledge, is not to-day more capable of analyzing the events of the past, than were those timorous souls of King James's day, who feared God would strike them dead for investigating his mysteries?

The fearless pioneer is yet to come in the Church, who will point out in a sensible way the shortest and best road to eternal peace, happiness on earth, and harmony hereafter. It is not to be gained by picturing hell and damnation, as punishment for those who differ from you, or do not believe in Christ as you picture him,—which God forbid they should,—but by giving Truth as it is.

THE SPIRIT-EDITOR'S VALEDICTORY.

JUDGE EDMONDS.

JUDGE EDMONDS, in life, was a man of quiet persistency of purpose, and possessed in a marked degree a keen, lawyer-like sagacity, which enabled him to penetrate the bearings of a case almost at first sight. He has displayed the same admirable qualities during the progress of this Work, which he superintended in *spirit*.

It was at his request that the MS. was taken to London for publication, as it is made up largely of English contributions, and he has, in the face of many difficulties, adhered to his course in this respect.

Mrs. Horn crossed the Atlantic three times, to London, on necessary business in connection with the production of this Work, and the Judge cheerfully gave his aid in making arrangements and removing difficulties.

He always formed one of the party on the introduction of new Spirit-*literati* to our *Soirées*, and his courteous manner and genial company made the *Séances* to be ever remembered, as the intellectual *conversaziones* we read of as occurring in the days of Johnson and Coleridge, or the French *Salons* of Madame Roland, or Madame de Staël.

Y work is now completed, and I here thank you, Mr. Horn, and the Medium, for the attention you have shown to the guests I have presented to you.

I have sought the aid of the most intellectual and competent individuals of the present century, for the purpose of representing to the public different phases of Spirit-life. Spiritualism is steadily progressing. Prophecies, made during the early years of its inception, are being fulfilled.

Old creeds are passing away. In the light of these new truths, it is impossible for man to retain the dark superstitions of the past.

The leading minds of Germany, France and England are awakening to the fact that the inhabitants of another world are knocking at their doors. The Church trembles for her mythological creeds, under the voice of this New Dispensation.

America has always taken the initiative in progressive movements, and this greatest event of the Nineteenth Century, which opens the great North-west passage to the Polar Sea of death, making it navigable, and unveiling the mysteries that have kept mankind in a state of fear and tremor for centuries, has been owing to her enterprise and spirit of investigation.

Every age has had its "MYSTERIES," which the priesthood have taught the people to believe were connected with their future state, that they might thereby strengthen their own power, and attain an influence over ignorant and superstitious minds, by professing to be the go-between, the exponents of these dread and sacred mysteries to the people, who were incompetent to fathom them.

Our mission is to enlighten Humanity, and to prove that the sacred mysteries of Christianity, like the superstitious beliefs in the past—attending the eclipse, the earthquake, and volcanic eruptions—are the result of simple laws, and not miracles to be received with unquestioning faith.

As to the occupation of Spirits: their mode of living;

their creeds and theories of life; statements given by different individuals in the Spirit-world will vary according to their development, their intelligence, and the position or locality they occupy in the Next World.

It is true that that Next World is the refined spirit of this one, and therefore somewhat similar, but no more similar than the early geological condition of the Earth, when it was unfit for the habitation of man, was, compared with the present condition of the globe.

The refining process had to take place in your sphere before man could exist: so likewise the Spirit-world has been refined to its present condition.

Many centuries from hence, Earth will be refined to conditions that will enable spirits to live in its atmosphere, visibly, whereas now we can make ourselves apparent but for a few moments.

There is a mistaken idea prevailing among many as to the different spheres in the Spirit-world. It is supposed that these spheres are strata or layers, one above the other. I inclined to that belief while I lived on earth, but have since discovered my error. A Spirit-world is a vast globe very many times larger than the earth. I cannot give the exact size. The different localities in this Spirit-world we term " spheres." Persons passing from earth, according to their development, are drawn to different sections of this immense globe, and the word " Gulf," that which Dives saw (as depicted in the Bible) which separated him from his companions, is the condition that existed in one locality remote from the others, and in that locality all individuals in need of reformation, all men from low dens, or evil-minded, undeveloped persons, are attracted by a fixed law. It is as much their home and native place as the Polar Region is the home of the Esquimaux. They may progress out of it, and develop by means of education, the same as a snail-eating Indian may grow out of his low state and grub-like condition into a higher and more civilized one.

But time and their own efforts, and no miracle, will produce that change and result. On earth there are many places where those live whom we call "earth-bound spirits." Their homes are in the mountain fastnesses, uninhabited islands, great prairies and plains, and in the Polar Regions. Extremes of cold and heat generate an interior spirit-atmosphere unknown to the chemistry of earth, and which is never marked on your thermometer or barometer.

A spirit community has inhabited the mountains of Asia and Africa, from the earliest existence of man. The historic mountains of Greece and Italy have had their spiritual residents, known to the clairvoyant Greeks and Romans, and depicted in the ancient Mythology. But as civilization advanced, and roads were made over the hills and valleys, earth-bound spirits deserted those mountains, forests and glens, for more neglected regions.

The practice of the Catholic Church in erecting a chapel or shrine and crucifix in lone districts inhabited by spirits, to exorcise so-called evil spirits, though regarded as a superstition, is based upon an instinctive perception of laws that govern the spirits between the two worlds; for the magnetism of living persons disturbs the rest and abode of spirits, and they are obliged to remove when their solitude becomes a place of general resort.

The Spirit-Editor's Valedictory. 239

During the Dark Ages, when Christianity taught men *cruelty* and not LOVE! in the times of Martyrdom and Inquisition, earth-bound spirits were nearly as barbarous as the savages and cannibals. The horrid vision related by Dante, and the pictures by mediæval monks and inspired painters, representing the tortures of the damned souls, were drawn from partially-clairvoyant visions of the condition of spirits, who passed from earth in the midst of rapine and murder, and the innumerable cruelties of that age, fertile in inventions for producing pain and anguish.

There is a spiritual meaning to every fable. Every creed, that has gained a place in the affections of mankind, has an interior spiritual significance based on the eternal principles of Truth ! and the pictures of after-life drawn by the Brahman, the Mahommedan, the Egyptians, Hebrews, Greeks, and Romans, contained this germ of spiritual truth. Language is symbolical, and the pictures of the soul's after-condition, represented by the Oriental writers of the Scriptures, are symbolical of mental states, and not actualities.

It is well-known to all observers, and students of medicine, that the soul is capable of experiencing more intense suffering than the body. Despair, remorse, and a desire for revenge, cause greater torment than pain inflicted upon the body, so that individuals resort to suicide and all species of bodily torment, to decrease the anguish of the soul.

Therefore, as the spirit becomes many more times susceptible to ecstatic pain or pleasure, when released from the body, the clairvoyant pictures of Heaven and Hell, as endured by the soul, are emblematic of states, and not veritable places; as, for instance, the Sea of Ice described by Dante, the Houri's heaven of the Mahommedan, or the burning lake of fire of the Christian.

We have now arrived at a point in the World's History, when practical knowledge has taken the place of ideal speculation. Plain Truth has usurped the Kingdom of Romance. A concurrent change has ensued in the World of Spirits. The angels or messengers from the Spirit-land no longer address the citizens of Earth in hyperbolic language, but in words terse and explicit, free from the metaphoric allusions employed by the Prophets of old, they give to mankind information relative to the NEXT WORLD, without adornment; describing a world of cause and effect, not a miraculous Heaven and Hell, unadapted to thinking and loving beings, but a spiritualized earth, for which mortal experience is given man, to adapt him to live in with pleasure or pain, according to development and the use here made of material advantages.

VISIT TO THE SPIRIT-WORLD.

A STRANGER.

This interesting description came unsought, and by an author unknown. The Medium has failed to obtain the name of the writer. If it interests the reader, as it has the transcriber, it cannot fail to carry conviction of its truth with it, and prove a fitting close to a work of such momentous interest to humanity as this, which we inscribe "*The Next World.*"

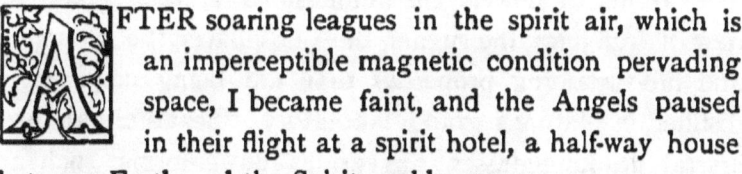FTER soaring leagues in the spirit air, which is an imperceptible magnetic condition pervading space, I became faint, and the Angels paused in their flight at a spirit hotel, a half-way house between Earth and the Spirit-world proper.

The building was circular in form, of white marble-like material, surmounted by several domes, not unlike the mosque of St. Sophia, or St. Mark's at Venice. It seemed to float in the air like a balloon, scintillated light like a star, filled my mind with wonder, not only from its magnificent portions, but from its artistic design.

We entered, and found collected thousands of travellers from all parts of the earth, being served with refreshments, under the different domes which I afterwards learned represented the various nations of the earth.

Young spirit-girls, dressed in a white lace-like material, stood about ready to talk with us, and give us advice, information, counsel, as we required it, and serve us, if that may be called serving, which consisted in merely touching some telegraphic fibre, which brought before us, on beautifully-ornamented dishes, the most delicious and nutritious food imaginable. As the tissues of a spirit's body are not gross like those of the earth-body, the food required to sustain life with them, is like the essence of earth-food. The aroma of flowers, the infinitesimal farina of grain, the dew of fruit-juice, the sugars, the phosphates, the albumen, and life-sustaining properties that are being continually distilled in Nature's grand laboratory. Beautifully-shaped crystal drinking-glasses of various flower-forms, such as lilies, tulips, and morning-glories, were passed to us filled with a pale yellow liquid, which tasted, as we imagined, like the ambrosial nectar of the Gods.

As I was curious to learn how spirits came by cups and goblets, one of the young maidens, of whom I have spoken, offered in response to my enquiry, to show me the wondrous process by which these "things of beauty" were constructed.

"In the first place," said my guide, "you must please remember, that form is designed by the spirit for use and beauty. All forms familiar to you on earth can be reproduced in the Spirit-world, because they are the result of spirit conception, clothed with matter, which is a means to make the spirit visible. The spiritual principle of matter becomes *visible matter* in the World of Spirits.

"The ancient Greek forms of vases and jars, so graceful and beautiful that they have been copied age after age, are but the expression of the old Greek artists' souls, solidified and made enduring. The process is eternal, for it is spiritual. We construct in the same manner that you do, only with more rapidity. Is not your earth and the whole planetary system but a materialized exhibition of the GREAT I AM's thought?

"Here, if you desire a dish ornamented in a certain manner, it will appear before your eyes. Why? Because your mind has been sufficiently educated, by contact with material substances, to enable you to give outward shape to your wish. Certain chemical combinations, volatile but eternal, produce sands and earths, which with heat and pressure result in giving to the inhabitants of earth the porcelain of Sevres and China, the ware of Dresden, the crystal of Venice, and the pottery of antiquity. Here, we produce the same type, more beautiful and by a quicker process. Follow me that you may learn."

I accompanied her to a room formed of different coloured crystals. In the centre stood a fountain, throwing its spray high in the air. A white, cream-like material filled the basin beneath it. On touching an electric thread, a portion of this clay rose upon a pedestal before me.

"Now," said my instructor, "place your hands upon this electrical battery, and wish distinctly for any form of cup, vase, or plate you may desire."

I followed the instructions given, and immediately there appeared upon the pedestal a very prettily-formed vase, of Greek design, which I had seen years before in a print; the very same shape I had had in my mind, when I touched the electric cord.

"How is this accomplished?" I asked.

"Thus: Your mind photographed the image of the Greek urn, and the electric power of your will acting upon the sensitive material, cut it as lightning splits a tree, but split it in the shape you designed in your mind.

"To the ignorant and uneducated mind, the process and result look like magic. They have not the art, education, or will-power, to produce, and more enlightened spirits produce for them, until they have finished their earth probation. For they are obliged to return to earth, and study in the art-studios and ateliers.

"In this Hotel, or 'Palace of Hospitality,' which is the spiritual meaning of hotel, we instruct travellers in the first principles of spirit-existence. This building was erected by a benevolent American and an English nobleman, worthy of his title, who, finding that birth into the Spirit-world was sometimes attended with as much loss and discomfort to the spirit as birth on earth is to the human being, without proper provision and forethought. Man needs to be cared for at his entrance on earth, so does his spirit on entering this world, to prevent its becoming dwarfed or cramped.

"In the barbarous ages, a great many spirits suffered untold misery, and the frightful pictures of Hell grew out of their experiences, in contending with the elements of an unknown world, and subject to attacks from cruel, undeveloped spirits.

"Christ's advent brought about a new era. He taught men to care for each other, so that when they entered the

Spirit-world they would feel an interest in their neighbour's welfare, and provide for their well-being. The man who despises his fellow-creatures becomes a pariah in Spirit-life.

"Do you see those moody spirits who come in and go out, wrapped in their own consciousness? They will not accept information from any one. They are those who are always denouncing mankind as bad; many are foolish Clergymen, Doctors of Divinity, rich men, titled Lords, and tyrannical land-holders.

"There are as many spirit-worlds as there are stars in heaven.

"Why is it necessary to teach morality and laws of justice, and to instruct men in being merciful, if there is no punishment or eternal torment for misdeeds?

"Because, there is no worse punishment than that which the dissatisfied soul makes for itself. Harmony, peace, refinement and mental culture, and effort to benefit the race, are the *Ultima Thule* of Humanity in the Spirit-world."

"But," said I, "all persons are not educated in refinement. In our country (America) in the back-woods, in the log cabins and farm houses, are many good fathers and mothers, who love to help the distressed, who have good hearts though they lack culture. They know how to get a dinner for the good man of the house, and the men know how to care for cattle and stock, but nothing more. Where is their place in a refined Spirit-world?"

"If life consisted in mere eating and drinking, in animal happiness, and not knowledge, they might continue for ever in the same plane of development; but spirit-life includes growth. No man can be thoroughly good without knowledge and experience. The placid goodness that brings individual ease, is not complete goodness. The spirit is one-sided, like that of the Brahman; it must be rounded."

"Christ taught," I replied, "that inasmuch as you do it to one of these little ones you do it to me."

"Oh yes! because that was active goodness inculcated, doing good to children. Unless you become as a little child, ready to learn, questioning but receptive, having confidence in mankind, you cannot enter the Kingdom of Heaven."

"I wish I could see Christ!" I exclaimed; a peculiar sort of fervour taking possession of me, bewildered with all I had seen and heard.

"Do you believe in such a being?" asked my guide. "There are many Saviours,—one Jesus Christ. Would you see him?"

"Yes!" I exclaimed, joyfully.

"I will take you to his city," said my companion. "It is in the Far East, near the rising sun; for though the whole world embraces his disciples, his abode is in the New Jerusalem, where the fields are ever green, and the streamlets limpid as crystal. Follow me: let us go."

Then out we spread our hands and feet, and floated through the air until we found ourselves over a vast city, surrounded by hills. The streets of the city, which were wide avenues circling it in many directions, looked like rivers of sunshine, as we hovered over the place before descending. Palms and olives, pomegranate, orange and citron trees, gave forth a delicious odour. Gardens of roses and lilies, and a strange shrub, to me unknown, spread forth great flowers, whose petals were crimson and purple, with golden centres. We alighted in the midst of a garden.

My mind seemed filled with the most sublime thoughts; delicious harmonies floated through my brain; every mote in the air looked like a golden star. I thrilled with strange ecstasy.

"What is the matter with me?" I asked my companion. "Why do I feel thus? I appear to comprehend life from the beginning of centuries. The world moves like a panorama before me. I feel an unutterable tenderness for humanity. I would gather the whole world into my arms!"

"It is the Christ atmosphere you drink in. It thrills your being. Thus we all feel when in the near presence of this wonderful man."

We moved on, and crossed a brook. A field of lilies, far as the eye could reach, stretched before us. In the midst of it I beheld a figure clothed in white raiment, belted around the waist in Oriental fashion. His face shone with a pale light, like moonlight upon the water. His dark hair was lit up by the halo, and his beautiful eyes seemed like orbs emitting rays of love. Falling upon me, my past life appeared to open like a scroll before them.

Seeing me trembling with emotion, he stretched out his hands, so beautifully formed, and, in a voice like strains of music, cried—

"Come unto me!"

Courage was given me, and I approached, sobbing.

"Oh! I feel that thou art the Christ."

"My daughter," said he, "like Mary, thou hast chosen the better part. Thou wouldst see him who would gather the whole world together as the hen gathers her brood under her wings."

"O Christ!" I answered, "I used to pray to thee when a little child, as my mother taught me, and since then I have prayed to thee in times of great trouble: Didst thou hear my prayer? Canst thou hear all the prayers that are said to thee, from all the churches of earth, from thousands and millions of lips?"

"Alas! child, the prayer of the formalist never reaches me. Few are the church prayers I hear. I listen, as after the rains and snows of winter you listen for the voice of the bird of early spring, so I listen for the heart prayers that come to me from that earth, swinging around still, half in darkness half in light: but the simple petition raised to me in love and faith, I hear and answer.

"Look there! seest thou that flower, just lifting its head above the others for a brief moment? that is a prayer. Some lone soul, abandoned and fainting, has cried: 'I know that Christ will help me! he will forgive me!' That person will feel the scent of that flower, like incense thrown over him to bless his life!"

"Wherever Christ steps," said my guide, "flowers spring up. As on earth you have seen persons with whom flowers thrive naturally, so the aura that Jesus emits produces these lovely blossoms, for it is like love and sunshine."

"O Christ!" I said: "Dost thou live always in this city? In all parts of Christendom: in England, France, Spain,

Russia, America, and the Islands of the Sea, people are worshipping thee. Dost thou keep apart from them, and dwell alone in this city and garden?"

An ineffable smile lighted his countenance as he replied:

"Child! those of whom thou speakest need me not. They worship not me. They worship their churches, their synagogues, their cathedrals, their robes and surplices, their priests, their incense, their choir boys, their meeting houses, their creeds—of Methodism, Presbyterianism, Baptism, and all the many 'Isms' that have been raised in my name; but Christ they do not worship. The principles that I taught, of love and forbearance, of living a life of intuition instead of externalism, they do not practise. When men learn to do good, regardless of forms, then will they be my disciples; for they will be the disciples of our Father God; the soul-principle of all that is of good.

"Behold the earth! how its people groan under burdens too grievous to be borne; how they are taxed to support a false God. Are those magnificent buildings, that dot the earth's surface, made to warm and house the homeless, to educate the ignorant, to comfort the poor and needy? No! they are erected for God and I, Jesus Christ.

"Do we live in them? Is not their odour unwholesome to our spirits? God is in the air. I am in the fields. I love the trees, the brooks, the flowers, and rocks. I dwell not in the great cathedrals. I pass by the churches built at the price of poverty's blood. But you can find me oft in the hovel, and many a lone suicide have I lifted out of the water and mire. Oh! my spirit is troubled, and I groan in anguish to see the wrongs that are practised in my name.

"Look around this beautiful city! it has been built by my early disciples, by the martyrs and believers in an undefiled religion; whose lives on earth made the earth better; who lived as I did, to lift humanity out of the teachings of narrow bigotry into the great river of Truth; by those who lived on earth long before my troubled life began : by Socrates, by Plato, Pythagoras, by Confucius, by Zoroaster, by Moses, and the priests and devotees of Egypt and India,—by all those who have endeavoured to elevate the soul of man above the animal plane."

"O Christ!" I cried, "we must have the means wherewith to do good. Thou didst not accomplish thy miracles without means. Thou hadst the water wherewith to make the wine. Thou hadst the loaves and fishes with which to increase the food of the multitude: so says the Word of God."

"The Word of God! my child : all history is the Word of God. The struggles of the human soul to attain perfection is a Bible, a sacred Book, written or unwritten. I became one with God, with the Great Spirit of the Universe. The miracles I wrought were the result of my silent study of Spiritual Law, which pervades the Universe of Natural Law, and which every medium or receptive soul can produce, by seeking aid of the Divine Father, the Spirit of Eternity."

"Dear Christ!" I here exclaimed, carried away by my thoughts : "May I ask if thou art indeed the Son of God? Is it all true that is said of thee, and wast thou born before thou didst appear on earth?"

As I asked this question, the flowers around Jesus

nodded their beautiful heads, and the air emitted a delicious odour.

"Yes! child, as all men who do the work of their Father in Heaven. No father on earth claimed me as his own, and in the poetical language of my country, I was the *child of God*. In all ages, the priests have put forth claimants of heavenly birth. Inspired by spirits, they have selected the best tools they could find to propagate a belief in Immortality. I was *not* an impostor: I was inspired of God; but the priests, my early instructors, hoped to inspire me to raise up an earthly kingdom, to rebel against the Government, and rouse my people to strike off the Roman chains that enthralled them. But the Kingdom, I was inspired to raise, was a spiritual one. Our people were in bondage to Mosaic laws, more galling than the Roman chains, because they had lost the spirit of those laws, and had become externalists. They taught that the Father of the Universe delighted in the sacrifice of bulls and goats, forgetting that Moses had instituted sacrificial ceremonies to teach them to be generous, and that what they best valued, their herds and their corn, should be devoted to elevate their spiritual natures.

"So blind were these blind leaders of the blind, that they taught that the Sabbath was for the especial use of this cruel God, and watched whether I would heal the sick on that day, that they might accuse me of breaking God's Law.

"Let every day be a Sabbath with thee, O my Father! and bring rest, and peace, and harmony, to the whole earth," cried Christ, stretching out his arms in benediction;

and as he spoke his breath seemed to warm up the distant earth, and a mellow glow spread over the whole face of the globe. The air was filled with music, as from human voices, from stringed instruments, and wind instruments, and the whole of nature; thrilling me with a wondrous joy, as though the millennium were come.

As I stood, entranced with what I had seen and heard, my guide touched me gently, saying :—

"Let us hasten back to earth, to inspire the mediums and teachers to help on the return of Christ to earth; that as he dwells in heaven he may yet dwell spiritually on earth, amid peace, plenty and harmony. On earth he was the incarnation of spiritual benevolence, the embodiment of the Divine afflatus : as we are the embodiment of all the thought of our ancestors, Christ was an embodiment of the Most High Spirit's thought. Oh ! that all men understood and obeyed the laws of the Universe, then would the earth be an Eden, and human beings possess the powers of Christ !"

PARK PLACE, SARATOGA SPRINGS, N.Y., Dec., 1883.

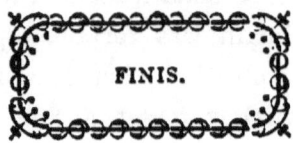

Foolscap, 8vo., 96 pp., Bound in Illustrated Boards with a Portrait of Mesmer, and embellished with

NINE PAGES OF ILLUSTRATIONS.

Price Two Shillings.

THE ILLUSTRATED
Practical Mesmerist:
CURATIVE AND SCIENTIFIC.
By WM. DAVEY.

Contents.

Physical and Mental Qualifications of the Operator—Age—Health—General Physical Adaptations—Mental Qualifications, &c., &c.—Practical Directions for Mesmerising—Favourable Circumstances — MEDICAL APPLICATION OF MESMERISM — Full Special Instructions for Treating Various Diseases — SCIENTIFIC APPLICATION OF MESMERISM — Rigidity—Fixing a Subject to the floor or in a chair—Mesmeric Concatenation—General Rigidity—Power of Will—Raising the Arms—Transmission of Sensation—Phreno-Mesmerism, and Practical Instructions for conducting experiments generally, &c., &c.

> The above Work has been out of print for many years, and has ranked amongst the foremost as a thoroughly Practical and Comprehensive Treatise on the subject. The publisher feels assured that its reappearance will be gratefully acknowledged, both by collectors of this class of literature and students of the Science, to whom it will prove very advantageous in forwarding their studies. Assisted by the Illustrations they will at once grasp that which would otherwise require hours of study. The Illustrations consist of nine full pages, carefully and artistically drawn, and executed in Litho. These represent the processes of Mesmerisation and Demesmerisation, Clairvoyance, Thought-Reading, Mesmerising Water, Second Sight, &c., &c. Bound up with the Book will be a Complete List of all obtainable Works on the Subject and its various phases, and the whole is published at the popular price of Two Shillings.

London: J. Burns, 15, Southampton Row.

Crown 8vo., 524 pp., Cloth, 8/-

Practical Instruction in Animal Magnetism.

By J. P. F. DELEUZE.
Translated by Thomas C. Hartshorn.

SUMMARY OF CONTENTS.

General Views and Principles—Of the Processes—Explanation of the word "Pass"—Effects commonly exhibited—Of Somnambulism, and the Uses to be made of it—Of Precaution in the Choice of Magnetiser—Application of Magnetism to Disease—Means of avoiding inconveniences and dangers—Of the means of developing in ourselves the Magnetic Faculty—The Practice and the Science, &c., &c.

** *A very exhaustive and reliable handbook*

Crown 8vo., 799 *pp. Cloth,* 14/-

Library of Mesmerism and Psychology:

IN ONE LARGE VOL. COMPRISING

The Philosophy of Mesmerism, Clairvoyance, and Medical Electricity—Fascination, or the Power of Charming—The Macrocosm, or the Universe Without—The Philosophy of Electrical Psychology—Doctrine of Impressions—Mind and Matter—Psychology, or the Science of the Soul.

James Burns, 15, Southampton Row, W.C.

SECOND EDITION. JUST PUBLISHED.

Foolscap 8vo., 120 pp., Illustrated. Price 1/-, *post free,* 1/2.

HOW TO MESMERISE.

BY

JAMES COATES.

A Manual of Instruction in the History, Mysteries, Modes of Procedure, and Arts of Mesmerism, or Animal Magnetism, Hypnotism-Clairvoyance, Thought-Reading, and Mesmeric Entertainments.

Summary of Contents.

CHAP. I.—Historical Outline.
„ II.—Modes of Procedure.
„ III.—Modes of Procedure (*continued*).
„ IV.—How to Mesmerise.
„ V.—Curative Mesmerism.
„ VI.—How to Give an Entertainment.
„ VII.—How to Give an Entertainment (*contd.*).
„ VIII.—Phreno-Mesmerism.
„ XI.—How to Mesmerise Animals.

16mo., 104 pp., *Illustrated, Paper,* 1/- *post free,* 1/1.

HOW TO MAGNETISE;

Or, Magnetism and Clairvoyance.

A Practical Treatise on the Choice, Management and Capabilities of Subjects, with Instruction on the Method of Procedure.

By JAMES VICTOR WILSON.

James Burns, 15, Southampton Row, W.C.

New Edition, Illustrated Cloth. **2/6**, *post free*, **2/8**.

MESMERISM,
Curative Magnetism and Massage.

With Nine full-page Illustrations, descriptive of the Mesmeric Passes.

BEING THE MESMERIC PORTION OF
"**The Magnetic & Botanic Family Physician.**"

BY

D. YOUNGER.

One of the most Comprehensive and Practical Works on the Subject, conveying by way of its Illustrations much valuable instruction to the student, not so readily elucidated in non-illustrated works.

Crown 8vo., 102 pp., Cloth, Red Edges, **2/6**.

Mesmerism, with Hints for Beginners.

By JOHN JAMES.

An excellent Text-Book by a Writer who has had Thirty Years' Experience in the Subject.

James Burns, 15, Southampton Row, W.C.

8vo., 378 pp., *Cloth, Illustrated,* 5/6.

ANIMAL MAGNETISM.

BY

ALFRED BINET and CHARLES FÉRÉ.

(Assistant Physician to the Salpêtrière.)

CONTENTS.

Animal Magnetism in its beginings: Mesmer and Puységur —History of Animal Magnetism: The Academic Period— History of Animal Magnetism: Braid—Hypnotism: Grimes, Azam, Durand de Gros, &c., &c. — Modes of Producing Hypnosis—Symptoms of Hypnosis—The Hypnotic States— Imperfect Forms of Hypnosis—General Study of Suggestion —Hallucinations—Suggestions of Movements and of Acts— Paralysis by Suggestions: Anæsthesia—Paralysis by Suggestion: Motor Paralysis—The Application of Hypnotism to Therapeutics and Education—Hypnotism and Responsibility.

Crown 8vo., 103 *pp., Cloth.* 2/6.

HYPNOTISM, or ANIMAL MAGNETISM.

Physiological Observations by RUDOLPH HEIDENHAIN, M.D.

Translated from the Fourth German Edition by

L. C. WOOLDRIDGE, M.D., D.Sc.

Crown 8vo., 60 *pp., Paper,* 6d., *post free,* 7d.

Six Lectures on the Philosophy of Mesmerism, or Animal Magnetism.

By Dr. John Bovee Dods.

Author of " *The Philosophy of Mesmerism and Electrical Psychology* "

James Burns, 15, Southampton Row, W.C.

Demy 8vo, between 500 *and* 600 *pp., Cloth.* **8/6.**

The Magnetic and Botanic Family Physician,

and Domestic Practice of Natural Medicine.

BY

D. YOUNGER.

with Illustrations Showing Various Phases of Mesmeric Treatment, including

Full and Concise Instructions in Mesmerism, Curative Magnetism, Massage, and Medical Botany; with a Complete Diagnosis of all Ordinary Diseases, and How to Treat them by Simple, Safe, and Natural Means; also Careful Directions for the Infusion of various Medicines and Tinctures; the Composition of Pills and Powders; Preparation of Medicated Oils, Salves, Liniments, Poultices, Toilet Requisites; all kinds of Bath and other Sanitary Appliances.

Crown 8vo., 203 *pp., Cloth,* **6/-**

Medical Electricity.

A Manual for Students, showing its most Scientific and Rational Application to all forms of Acute and Chronic Disease, by the different combinations of Electricity, Galvanism, Electro-Magnetism, etc., etc., and Human Magnetism.

By WILLIAM WHITE, M.D.

Crown 8vo., 214 *pp., Cloth.* **3/6.**

Healing by Faith.

Or, Primitive Mind Cure. The Nature and Power of Faith; or Elementary Lessons in Christian Philosophy and Transcendental Medicine.

By W. F. EVANS.

James Burns, 15, Southampton Row, W.C.

Crown 8vo., Paper Wrappers **21/-**, *binding from* **4/-** *extra.*
(*Third Edition.*)

Practical Instructions
IN THE
Science and Art of Organic Magnetism.

By MISS CHANDOS LEIGH HUNT
(Mrs. Wallace.)

Being her Original Three-Guinea Work greatly enlarged and carefully revised by the Authoress.

The above Work is an epitome of all the best and most reliable works on the subject and as such is a standard book of reference and instruction.

8vo., Paper, **2/-**

MESMERISM, SPIRITUALISM, WITCHCRAFT AND MIRACLES.

A Treatise, showing that Mesmerism is a Key which will unlock many Chambers of Mystery.

By ALLEN PUTNAM.

8vo., 32 pp., Paper, **1/-**

ON MESMERISM.
By A. P. SINNETT.

This Pamphlet forms an admirable Introduction to the Study of Mesmerism.

James Burns, 15, Southampton Row, W.C.

8vo., Cloth, post free, 5/-

Vital Magnetic Cure.

By A MAGNETIC PHYSICIAN.

Showing the Natural, Electric, Magnetic and Spiritual Life-Forces that Control the Human Organism, and the Application of these Forces to Relieve all Forms of Curable Disease—Mental and Physical.

This is a most comprehensive and compact exposition, in a perfectly intelligible form, of the virtue of the magnetic forces in individuals, and the many modes in which they act and interact in ordinary life. It contains some practical suggestions on healing the sick, from the pen of a well-known doctor of divinity, the late Rev. ELIAKIM PHELPS; also an Essay that was written by and through his son while entranced.

Cloth, post free, 6/6.

Mental Cure.

By W. F. EVANS.

Illustrating the Influence of the Mind on the Body, both in Health and Disease, and the Psychological Method of Treatment.

The design of this original treatise is to explain the nature and laws of the inner life of man, and to contribute some light on the subject of Mental Hygiene, which is beginning to assume importance in the treatment of disease, and to attract the attention of physiologists. The author has aimed to illustrate the correspondence of the soul and body, their mutual action and reaction, and to demonstrate the casual relation of disordered mental states to diseased physiological action, and the importance and mode of regulating the intellectual and affectional nature of the invalid under any system of medical treatment.

James Burns, 15, Southampton Row, W.C.

8vo., 328 pp., Cloth, post free, **7/6.**

Statuvolence ;
Or, ARTIFICIAL SOMNAMBULISM.
Hitherto called Mesmerism, or Animal Magnetism.
By William Baker Fahnestock, M.D.
Containing a brief historical survey of Mesmer's operations, and the examination of the same by the French commissioners; Phreno-Somnambulism, Phreno-Mesmerism and Neurology; The Proper Method of Preparing Subjects for Surgical Operations; Management during and after the same, &c., &c.

8vo., 128 pp., Paper, post free, **2/6.**

Full and Comprehensive Instructions
HOW TO MESMERIZE.
Ancient and Modern Miracles by Mesmerism. Also, Is Spiritualism True?
By Prof. J. W. Cadwell.
Ancient and Modern Miracles are explained by Mesmerism, and the book will be found highly interesting to every Spiritualist. It is the only work ever published giving full instruction How to Mesmerize, and the connection this Science has with Spiritualism. It is pronounced by Allen Putnam and others, who have read it, to be one of the most interesting books ever written.

Large 8vo., 322 pp., Handsome Cloth, Illustrated, **8/6.**

The Modern Bethesda ;
Or, The Gift of Healing Restored.
By A. E NEWTON.
Being some account of the Life and Labours of Dr. J. R. NEWTON, Healer, with observations on the nature and source of the Healing Power, and the condition of its exercise. Notes on valuable Auxiliary Remedies, Health Maxims, etc.

James Burns, 15, Southampton Row, W.C.

Crown 8vo., 176 pp., Cloth 4/-

Fascination;
Or, the Philosophy of Charming.

Illustrating the Principles of Life in connection with Spirit and Matter.

By JOHN B. NEWMAN, M.D.

Limp Cloth. Price. 1/-
THE REVIVED
Ancient Art of Massage.

A Powerful Therapeutic Agent in the Cure of Disease without the Aid of Medicine.

By EDWARD WILLIAMS.

Paper, price 9d.
Private Instructions in Practical Massage.
By Dr. J. D. Balkam.

This work is devoted to explaining the Method of Curing Disease by Massage Treatment, or Hand Manipulation, and is full of useful suggestions to the suffering.

Paper 2d., *Post free,* 2½d.
CLAIRVOYANCE.
By ADOLPHE DIDIER.

NOTICE.

☞ Zinc and Copper Discs.

Of great assistance in producing the Mesmeric Sleep.
Well made and finished, 4/- *per doz.*

James Burns, 15, Southampton Row, W.C.

MR. BURNS can generally supply Secondhand Copies of the undermentioned Rare and Standard Works on Mesmerism, now out of print, and mentioned by Miss Chandos Leigh Hunt in her work "Practical Instructions in the Science and Art of Organic Magnetism," 21s.—*(See Page 7 of this Catalogue)* :—

A Practical Manual of Animal Magnetism, by A. Teste. 7/6. 1843

Animal Magnetism (Mesmerism) and Artificial Somnambulism : being a Complete and Practical Treatise on that Science, by Countess C *** de St. Dominique. 7/6. 1874

Facts in Mesmerism, with Reasons for a Dispassionate Enquiry into it, by Rev. Chauncy H. Townshend, A.M. Second edition, 7/6. 1844

Animal Magnetism and Magnetic Lucid Somnambulism, by E. Lee, M.D. 7/6. 1866

The Mighty Curative Powers of Mesmerism, by Thomas Capern. 6/- 1851

Natural and Mesmeric Clairvoyance, by J. Esdaile. 8/6. 1852

Somnolism and Psycheism, by J. W. Haddock. 7/6. 1851

Human Magnetism, by W. Newnham. 5/- 1845

Etherology and the Phreno-Philosophy of Mesmerism and Magic Eloquence, by J. Stanley Grimes. 6/- 1850

Physico-Physiological Researches in the Dynamics of Magnetism, Electricity, &c., &c., by Reichenbach. Gregory's translation, 16/-; Ashburner's translation, half calf, 21/.

FULL CATALOGUE OF CURIOUS AND INTERESTING BOOKS ON SPIRITUALISM, OCCULTISM, &c., FREE ON APPLICATION.

James Burns, 15, Southampton Row, W.C.

16th *thousand.* *Paper,* 6d.; *Cloth,* 1/-

Illness: Its Cause & Cure.

Showing How to Preserve Health and Cure Diseases by a Safe, Scientific, Pleasant and Efficient Means within the reach of all.

How to Preserve Health is a matter of no small importance, nor is it an Utopian undertaking. Nearly all diseases are preventible, and the fraction of time and money spent in acquiring the necessary knowledge is insignificant compared with the loss and suffering incurred by ill-health, doctors, and drugs.

How to Cure Disease Normally is indicated by the means required to preserve health. Such modes of cure are:—

Safe,—being in accordance with the laws of health, they cannot possibly destroy the patient or undermine the constitution, as the common practice of administering poison does.

Scientific. The remedies propounded in this book are based upon the *nature of disease*, and the demands of the system in respect to regaining the normal condition. Hence dangerous courses of experiments are superseded by a certain means producing the desired result. This practical knowledge will prove the death-blow to all kinds of medical quackery and malpractice.

Pleasant are such means and grateful to the diseased condition as food is to the hungry, drink to the thirsty, or rest to the weary. No disgusting draughts, painful operations, or enfeebling processes, but the whole is regenerating and restorative.

Efficient in all cases where cure is possible, is this system. Under it acute diseases, small-pox, fevers, diphtheria, bronchitis, rheumatism, &c., and all common ailments lose their virulent character ; and by observing the rules of health laid down, they might be banished from the land, and with them the dreaded cholera.

These means are within the reach of all. The poorest in the land may understand the system and avail themselves of its blessings. Sanitary associations should be formed in each town and missionaries employed to teach it to those who cannot read and investigate these simple phenomena for themselves.

Send 7 stamps for a sample copy at once, while you are well, and do all you can to spread it amongst your friends.

James Burns, 15, Southampton Row, W.C.

IMPORTANT AMERICAN WORK.

SEXUAL PHYSIOLOGY:

A Scientific and Popular Exposition
of the
Fundamental Principles in Sociology.

BY

R. T. TRALL, M.D.

Printed on Fine Paper. strongly bound in Cloth, 5/-

It contains Sixteen Chapters. extending over 312 pages, illustrated by Eighty Engravings; gives the complete Anatomy and Physiology of the Sexual Organs, Origin of Life, and everything connected with Impregnation and Generation, according to the latest Discoveries in Science.

These topics are treated from a scientific and elevated standpoint. The position of the Author in the medical world (not being a drug doctor) precludes the chance of quackery. There are no disgusting details of diseases nor immoral associations, but just such useful, aye, and indispensable information as would enable many well-meaning men and women to afford to each other and to posterity the obligations which the closest and most endearing associations demand. There is no relationship so important as that which underlies the formation of a new being, and there is none in which there is so much popular ignorance and abuse. This, then, is a work of the greatest importance, and should be widely diffused by all lovers of morality and human progress.

James Burns, 15, Southampton Row, W.C.

STANDARD WORK ON MESMERISM.
New Edition. — Just Published. — Post Free, 3/6.

THE
Philosophy of Mesmerism
and
Electrical Psychology.

BY
JOHN BOVEE DODS.

Comprised in Two Courses of Lectures, Eighteen in Number. Complete in One Volume. Including the Lecture on
"THE SECRET REVEALED. by which all may know how to Experiment without an Instructor."
EDITED by J. BURNS.

(The American Editions, in Two Vols., sell at Eight Shillings.)

CONTENTS.
PHILOSOPHY OF MESMERISM.

LECT. I. Introductory Lecture on Animal Magnetism.—II. Mental Electricity, or Spiritualism.—III. An Appeal in behalf of the Science.—IV. The Philosophy of Clairvoyance.—V. The Number of Degrees in Mesmerism.—VI. Jesus and the Apostles.

THE PHILOSOPHY OF ELECTRICAL PSYCHOLOGY.

DEDICATION.—INTRODUCTION.—LECT. I. Electrical Psychology: Its Definition and Importance in Curing Diseases.—II. Beauty of Independent Thought and Fearless Expression.—III. Connecting Link between Mind and Matter, and Circulation of the Blood.—IV. Philosophy of Disease and Nervous Force.—V. Cure of Disease and being Acclimated.—VI. Existence of Deity proved from Motion.—VII. Subject of Creation Considered.—VIII. Doctrine of Impressions.—IX. Connection between the Voluntary and Involuntary Nerves.—X. Electro-Curapathy is the best Medical System in being, as it involves the excellencies of all other systems.—XI. The Secret Revealed, so that all may know how to Experiment without an Instructor.—XII. Genetology, or Human Beauty Philosophically Considered.

James Burns, 15, Southampton Row, W.C.

List of Cheap Handbooks and Appliances for the Study of the Elements of Phrenology.

CHARTS.

SYMBOLICAL HEAD AND PHRENOLOGICAL CHART, consisting of a Coloured Head, 9×6 in. with illustrated divisions and definitions of the various developments; also seven additional engravings, showing the positions of the organs and brain. Every organ is appropriately illustrated and numbered so that the student may refer to the descriptive letterpress. Beautifully coloured, post free, 6½d.

A SIMILAR CHART, printed in Litho, and mounted for hanging, post free, 1/9.

A MAP OF THE HEAD, showing the cranial surface of the cerebral organs. 4d., or superfine paper, 6d.

BUSTS.

In Plaster, with all the developments marked— 1/- 2/-, 3 6. 6-; Or, THE IMPROVED CHINA BUST, with upwards of 100 Divisions, 10/6. Packing and carriage extra.

HANDBOOKS.

FOWLER'S NEW ILLUSTRATED SELF-INSTRUCTOR in Phrenology and Physiology. Illustrated, 2/-

THE FACE AS INDICATIVE OF CHARACTER. Being a Series of Chapters on Physiognomy. Edited by A. T. STORY. Illustrated by 120 portraits. Paper, 2/-; cloth, 3/-

A MANUAL OF PHRENOLOGY. By A. T. STORY. Numerous Illustrations, 1/-, cloth, 1/6.

FAMILIAR LESSONS ON PHRENOLOGY. Designed for the Use of Children and Youth. By Mrs. L. N. FOWLER. 6d.

HOW TO LEARN PHRENOLOGY. By L. N. FOWLER. A demand having arisen for something in a cheap and simple form for beginners, this little work has been prepared with a view to providing for this want. 6d.

THE PHRENOLOGICAL AND PHYSIOLOGICAL REGISTER. By L. N. FOWLER. Contains the definitions of the newly-discovered organs and sub-divisions marked on the new bust. 4d.

A CHAPTER ON NOSES. Profusely Illustrated. 6d.

THE MOUTH AND LIPS. 6d.

THE EYES AND EYEBROWS. 6d.

James Burns, 15, Southampton Row, W.C.

Royal 16mo., 108 pp., handsome cloth, 1/6;
extra gilt, 2/6.

THE ECONOMY
OF HUMAN LIFE.

SAID TO BE TRANSLATED FROM AN

Indian Manuscript written by an Ancient Brahmin.

The Best Reading Book for Spiritual Meetings, Public
or Private.

A Suitable Prize for Lyceum Children. Special Terms for Quantities.

GERALD MASSEY'S LECTURES.
ONE SHILLING EACH.

1—**The Historical (Jewish) Jesus** and the Mythical (Egyptian) Christ.
2—**Paul as a Gnostic Opponent,** not the Apostle of Historic Christianity.
3—**The Logia of the Lord;** or, the Pre-Christian Sayings ascribed to Jesus the Christ.
4—**The Devil of Darkness;** or, Evil in the Light of Evolution.
5—**Man in Search of His Soul,** during Fifty Thousand Years, and How He Found It.
6—**The Seven Souls of Man,** and their Culmination in Christ.
7—**Gnostic and Historic Christianity.**
8—**Luniolatry: Ancient and Modern.**
9—**The Hebrew Creations Fundamentally** Explained.
10—**The Coming Religion.**

James Burns, 15, Southampton Row, W.C.

Works on the Phenomena and Philosophy of Spiritualism.

THE COMPLETE WORKS OF ANDREW JACKSON DAVIS.
Comprising Twenty-seven Uniform Volumes, all neatly Bound in Cloth.

HISTORY AND PHILOSOPHY OF EVIL. 3s. 6d.   *Postage* 3d.
HARBINGER OF HEALTH. 6s. 6d.   „ 5d.
HARMONIAL MAN, OR THOUGHTS FOR THE AGE. 3s. 6d.   2d.
EVENTS IN THE LIFE OF A SEER. (Memoranda.) 6s. 6d.   5d.
PHILOSOPHY OF SPECIAL PROVIDENCES. 3s.   „ 2d.
FREE THOUGHTS CONCERNING RELIGION. 3s. 6d.   „ 3d.
PENETRALIA, CONTAINING HARMONIAL ANSWERS. 7s. 6d.   5d.
PHILOSOPHY OF SPIRITUAL INTERCOURSE. 6s.   „ 5d.
THE INNER LIFE, OF SPIRIT MYSTERIES EXPLAINED. 6s. 6d.   5d.
THE TEMPLE—ON DISEASES OF BRAIN AND NERVES. 6s. 6d.   5d.
THE FOUNTAIN, WITH JETS OF NEW MEANINGS. 4s. 6d.   3d.
TALE OF A PHYSICIAN, OR SEEDS AND FRUITS OF CRIME. 4s. 6d.   „ 3d.
THE SACRED GOSPELS OF ARABULA. 5s.   „ 2d.
DIAKKA, AND THEIR EARTHLY VICTIMS. 3s   „ 2d.
NATURE'S DIVINE REVELATIONS. 15s.   „ 6d.
THE PHYSICIAN. Vol. I. Great Harmonia. 6s. 6d.   „ 5d.
THE TEACHER.   „ II.   „   6s. 6d.   „ 5d.
THE SEER.   „ III.   „   6s. 6d.   „ 5d.
THE REFORMER.   „ IV.   „   6s. 6d.   „ 5d.
THE THINKER.   „ V.   „   6s. 6d.   „ 5d.
THE MAGIC STAFF: AN AUTOBIOGRAPHY OF A. J. DAVIS. 7s. 6d.   „ 5d.
BEYOND THE VALLEY: Sequel to "The Magic Staff." 6s. 6d.   5d.
A STELLAR KEY TO THE SUMMER LAND. 3s. 6d.   „ 3d.
ARABULA, OR THE DIVINE GUEST. 6s. 6d.   „ 4d.
APPROACHING CRISIS, OR TRUTH *v.* THEOLOGY. 4s. 6d.   4d.
ANSWERS TO EVER-RECURRING QUESTIONS FROM THE PEOPLE. 6s. 6d.   „ 5d.
DEATH AND THE AFTER-LIFE. 3s. 6d.   „ 3d.
THE PHILOSOPHY OF DEATH. (New Edition.)   Price 2d.
DEATH IN THE LIGHT OF THE HARMONIAL PHILOSOPHY. 1d.

James Burns, 15, Southampton Row, W.C.

Now Ready. 8vo., 252 pp., *handsome cloth gilt*, 5/-

THE NEXT WORLD.

By the Spirit-Editors:— Margaret Fuller (Contessa Ossoli), and Judge Edmonds.

BEING A COMPANION VOLUME TO "STRANGE VISITORS."

By SUSAN G. HORN, Clairvoyante.

Containing the following Essays and Papers by Individuals now dwelling in Spirit-Life.

ENGLAND AND THE QUEEN. By Prince Albert.
SKETCH OF LIFE IN THE SPIRIT-WORLD. By Harriet Martineau.
HOME OF HORACE GREELEY. By Horace Greeley.
EVOLUTION. By Professor Agassiz.
IMMORTALITY. By John Stuart Mill.
INTERVIEW WITH EDWIN FORREST.
METEMPSYCHOSIS, By Lord Lytton.
TWO CHRISTMAS CAROLS. By Charles Dickens.
THE STORY OF THE GREAT KING. By Hans Christian Andersen.
CHATEAU IN THE MIDST OF ROSES. By George Sands.
AN OPIUM-EATER'S DREAM OF HEAVEN. By De Quincey.
SPIRIT-FLOWERS. By Fanny Fern.
STATESMANSHIP FROM A SPIRITUAL STANDPOINT. By Secretary Seward.
THE SPIRIT-BRIDE. By Mrs. Gaskell.
RICH MEN OF NEW YORK: VANDERBILT. By Judge Edmonds.
PERSONAL EXPERIENCES. By George Smith, Assyriologist.
MY PASSAGE TO SPIRIT-LIFE. By Abraham Lincoln.
DEATH BY FIRE. By Charlotte Cushman.
REFORM IN SPIRIT-LIFE. By Charles Kingsley, Author of "Alton Locke."
LONE STAR: AN INDIAN NARRATIVE, By Fennimore Cooper.
ART NOTES. By Titian.
LEAVES FROM MY JOURNAL. By Dr. Livingstone.
PRE-HISTORIC RACES OF MAN. By Herodotus.

Its purpose is to teach the great truths of Spirit-Life as expressed in the desire of its Spirit-Editor. It is the work of spirits who on the earth-plane attained to great eminence; and these communications from them in spirit-life are well worthy of their earthly reputation. This book will make a greater stir amongst the intellectual classes than any that have preceded it.

James Burns, 15, Southampton Row, W.C.

(A MOST LEARNED AND INTERESTING WORK.)
Neat Wrapper, 1/-

On the Connection of Christianity with Solar Worship.

TRANSLATED FROM THE FRENCH OF DUPIUS, BY T. E. PARTRIDGE.

CONTENTS.

Allegorical Nature of the Hebrew Scriptures. Opinions of the Christian Fathers, The Story of the Creation is symbolical.
The Hebrew Cosmogony is borrowed from the Persian.
Persian and Christian Theology compared.
Origin of the idea of good and evil Deities.
Theology derived from Astronomy.
What the Serpent signifies in Theology.
The meaning of the Virgin Mother and her Child.
Correspondence between Egyptian and Roman Myths.
The Mithraitic Religion described.
The Blood of the Lamb, its signification.
Identity of Christ, Horus, and the Sun.
Assumption of the Virgin, what it means. The origin of Easter.
The Resurrection of Christ. The dragon and lamb of the Apocalypse.
The lamb a symbol of Christ. Why?
Redemption and Restoration under the Lamb.
Sun Worship in Egypt—Osiris. Parallels between Osiris and Christ.
The Phœnician Idea of Christ. Adonis and Christ compared.
Similarity of the Gods of Egypt and Greece.
The Phrygian God, Atys. The God Atys compared with Christ.
Coincidence of Christianity with Paganism.
Light, the great Divinity of all Nations.
The Christian Sacraments borrowed from Persia.
The Sympathy of Religions—Christian Redemption an Allegory.
The Spiritual meaning of ancient mysteries.
Authors, Ancient and Modern, noted:—

Archbishop Burnet, Maimonides, Philo, Origen, Cedrenus, Josephus, Beausobre, Clement, Augustine, Zoroaster, Strabo, Plutarch, Poock, Abulfeda, Manilius, Geminus, Pliny, Hyde, Virgil, Abulferaglus, Syncellus, Cyril, St. John, Macrobius, Proclus, Eratosthenes, Father Petau, Emperor Julian, St. Justin, Tertullian, Porphyry, Celsus, Montfaucon, Torre, Kirker, Freret, Abulmazar, Selden, Pic, Roger Bacon, Albert the Great, Stoffler, Columella, Ptolemy, Epiphanius, Theophanes, Theodore of Gaza, Isidore, St. Jerome, Martianus Capella, Pope Adrian, St. Paul, Athanasius, Eusebius, Diodorus, Diogenes Laertius, Procopius, Vossius, Suidas, Cheremon, Abnephius, Synesius, Theophilus, Athenagoras, Minutius Felix, Lactantius, Julius Firmicus, Herodotus, Arnobius, Pausanias, Ammianus Marcellinus, Corsini, Damascius, Varro, Sallust, Theodoret, Chrysostom: Jews, Manicheans, Essenians, Therapeutæ, Rabbis, Persians, Allegorists, Christians, Catholics, Assyrians, Ninevites, Magi, Romans, Greeks, Neapolitans, Egyptians, Phrygians, Brahmins, Phœnicians, Scythians, Bythinians, Arabians,

---

James Burns, 15, Southampton Row, W.C.

Demy 4to., 196 pp., handsome bevelled boards, **6/-,** *postage 9d.*

Embellished with Thirty-two Engravings, and Eight Chromo-lithographs.

'TWIXT TWO WORLDS.

A NARRATIVE OF THE
Life and Work of William Eglinton.

By JOHN S. FARMER.

THE above is one of the most valuable contributions to the literature of Spiritualism, conveying by way of its numerous illustrations a complete knowledge of that most interesting and startling phase of Spirit manifestation—MATERIALISATION, and records of wonderful Psychographic Seances given by the same medium.

2nd Edition, 8vo., 603 pp., handsome cloth gilt, Illus., **8/6.**

Startling Facts in Modern Spiritualism.

With a Graphic Account of Spirit Phenomena that have occurred in Europe and America, since March 31, 1848, to the Present Time.

By N. B. Wolfe, M.D.

Large 8vo., 265 pp., bevelled boards, Illustrated, **3/6.**

Transcendental Physics.

An Account of Experimental Investigations. From the Scientific Treatises of J. C. F. ZOLLNER, Professor of Physical Astronomy at the University of Leipsic, etc. Translated from the German, with a Preface and Appendices, by C. C. MASSEY, Barrister-at-law.

16mo., 120 pp., handsome cloth gilt, **2/-** *post free.*

CONCERNING SPIRITUALISM.

By GERALD MASSEY.

James Burns, 15, Southampton Row, W.C.

Large 8vo., 402 pp., Cloth, 5/-

Report on Spiritualism.

BY THE

COMMITTEE OF THE LONDON DIALECTICAL SOCIETY.

Being a Report in full, of the Opinions and Experiences of the Clergymen, Barristers, Solicitors, Physicians, Surgeons, Editors, Litterati, Scientists, Merchants, and others forming the Investigating Committee, as presented by them to the Society, after an investigation extending over many months, recording extraordinary Spiritual Phenomena, directly attested. It is the most complete and useful work on Spiritualism, and should be obtained by all interested in the subject.

8vo., 528 pp., bevelled boards, 7/6.

Essays from the Unseen.

DELIVERED THROUGH THE MOUTH OF W.L., A SENSITIVE.

RECORDED by A.T.T.P.

Containing 18 Oriental Controls; 22 Ancient Greek and Roman Controls; 11 Miscellaneous Controls; 18 Controls of the Renaissance, together with an Introductory Chapter, &c., and Ink-Photo Illustrations of the RECORDER, and fac-similes of Drawings done by the Sensitive, of "Thomas Paine," "Julian," and "Busiris."

Small 8vo., 199 pp., Paper, 1/6.

Facts and Fantasies.

By H. SPICER.

A SEQUEL TO

SIGHTS AND SOUNDS, THE MYSTERY OF THE DAY.

We have secured the remaining copies of this work which has been long out of print.

8vo., 358 pp., cloth, 3/6.

Letters and Tracts on Spiritualism.

By JUDGE EDMONDS.

Memorial Edition, with Memoir and Passing Away of the Author; and Discourses by T. Parker and Judge Edmonds, through MRS. TAPPAN.

James Burns, 15, Southampton Row, W.C.

8vo., 483 pp., handsome cloth, published at 7/6.
Now Reduced to 5/-

DISCOURSES Through the MEDIUMSHIP

OF

Mrs. CORA L. V. TAPPAN (Richmond).

THE NEW SCIENCE.
SPIRITUAL ETHICS, &c., &c.

Containing upwards of 50 Orations and Poems delivered in London during 1874 and 1875, descriptive of Facts concerning the Spirit-world, and communion between it and the Earth-plane.

Ornamented cloth gilt, second edition, enlarged, 2/6.

Experiences in Spiritualism:

A Record of Extraordinary Phenomena witnessed through the most Powerful Mediums, with some Historical Fragments relating to SEMIRAMIDE, given by the Spirit of an Egyptian who lived contemporary with her.

BY

CATHERINE BERRY.

CONTENTS:—A Paper read at the Spiritual Institution—Spiritual Phenomena: Seances at Home—Seances in Public—Spirit-Drawings—Spirit Prophecies of the War—Healing Mediumship—Materialisation of the Spirit-Form—Spirit Photography—Historical Fragments relating to Semiramide.

James Burns, 15, Southampton Row, W.C.

(*Very Scarce*, 1845.) 12mo., 338 pp., *cloth*, **10/6**.
Or Handsomely Bound in Half Calf extra, 12s 6d

THE SEERESS OF PREVORST.
By MRS. CROWE.
(Authoress of "THE NIGHT SIDE OF NATURE," &c. &c.)

Being the Revelations concerning the Inner-life of Man, and the Inter-Diffusion of a World of Spirits in the one we inhabit.

Communicated by Justinus Kerner. From the German by Mrs Crowe.

This book should be known and read more widely among modern Spiritualists. The occurrences which it chronicles antedate the American outpouring of psychic power by twenty years at least. It relates the revelations communicated to the world through the trance-mediumship of a very remarkable woman, who was the subject of spiritual manifestations from her earliest years, and of whom, upon one occasion, an extraordinary suspension of gravity is recorded. The development of the sun-sphere and of the life-sphere within the sceress, speaking in an unknown tongue, the religious signification of the spheres, the unveiling of the solar system to the liberated spirit of the clairvoyante, the relation of the divine and immortal spirit to the soul and body of the individual man, the magnetic man in his approximation to the world of spirits, an interesting theory of ghost-seeing—these are the subjects discussed in this wonderful history, whose authenticity is almost established from the mere character of its author. "The sincerity and good faith of Dr. Kerner in this affair," says Mrs. Crowe, "has never, we believe, been impugned, even by the most determined sceptic. He is well known in Germany as an exceedingly sensible, amiable, and religious man; and is a lyric poet of considerable eminence."

8vo., 252 pp., *cloth*, **5/-**
STUDIES OF THE OUTLYING FIELDS OF PSYCHIC SCIENCE.
A NEW BOOK by HUDSON TUTTLE.

The subjects treated are as follows:—What the Senses Teach of the World and the Doctrine of Evolution; Scientific Methods in the Study of Man and its Results; What is the Sensitive State? Mesmerism, Hypnotism, Somnambulism; Clairvoyance, Sensitiveness Proved by Psychometry; Sensitiveness during Sleep; Dreams; Sensitiveness Induced by Disease; Thought Transference; Intimations of an Intelligent Force Beyond Superior to the Actor; Effect of Psychical Conditions on the Sensitive; Unconscious Sensitiveness,&c.

James Burns, 15, Southampton Row, W.C.

SECOND EDITION, JUST PUBLISHED, HANDSOME CLOTH,
LARGE OCTAVO, ILLUSTRATED, 16/6 POST FREE.

THE HIDDEN WAY ACROSS THE THRESHOLD.

OR, THE MYSTERY WHICH HATH BEEN HIDDEN FOR AGES AND FROM GENERATIONS.

An Explanation of the Concealed Forces in Every Man to Open the Temple of the Soul and to Learn

THE GUIDANCE OF THE UNSEEN HAND.

BY J. C. STREET, A.B.N.

(Fellow of the Order S.S.S., and of the Brotherhood Z.Z.R.R.Z.Z.)

The Book is full Octavo size, contains over 600 pages, illustrated and printed with large, plain type, and its manufacture is First Class in every way, giving more Light and Knowledge of Spirit Ways and Occult Science than all previous works in English have done.

8vo., 316 pp., handsome cloth, 3/6 post free.

INSPIRATIONAL LECTURES AND IMPROMPTU POEMS.

Delivered by W. J. COLVILLE, in London; with a Personal Sketch of the Speaker.

Seven Steps to Spiritual Perfection—The Coming of the Kingdom of God—Spiritualism and its Relations to Theosophy and Christianity—The Philosophy of Re-embodiment—The True Gift of Healing—True Spiritual Marriage, &c., &c.

8vo., Cloth, 5/-

SPIRITUAL, ETHICAL and HISTORICAL DISCOURSES.

Delivered under Inspiration by W. J. COLVILLE, in Berkeley Hall, Boston, U.S.A.

The Problem of Prayer—Who and what is God?—Temples of the Living God—The Problem of Good and Evil—Esoteric Buddhism—Mediums and Mediumship—Spirit Materialisation—Jesus of Nazareth—Atlantis, &c., &c.

James Burns, 15, Southampton Row, W.C.

EMINENT SCIENTIFIC WORK ON SPIRITUALISM.

Large 8vo., Handsome Ornamented Cloth, Gilt, 5/-

With 16 Illustrations of Appliances for the Scientific demonstration of the genuineness of the Phenomena, including Portrait of Mr. D. D. Home holding the accordion under the table while it was being played on by the agency.

RESEARCHES
IN
THE PHENOMENA OF SPIRITUALISM.

BY

WILLIAM CROOKES, F.R.S., &c.

(*Embodying the following Treatises reprinted from the "Quarterly Journal of Science"*)

I.

"SPIRITUALISM VIEWED BY THE LIGHT OF MODERN SCIENCE," and "EXPERIMENTAL INVESTIGATIONS ON PSYCHIC FORCE."

With 16 Illustrations and Diagrams, proving beyond all doubt the reality of the Phenomena.

II.

"PSYCHIC FORCE AND MODERN SPIRITUALISM."

A Reply to the *Quarterly Review* and other critics, to which is added Correspondence upon Dr. Carpenter's asserted Refutation of the Author's Experimental Proof of the Existence of a hitherto Undetected Force, with two Illustrations.

III.

"NOTES OF AN INQUIRY INTO THE PHENOMENA CALLED SPIRITUAL, DURING THE YEARS 1870-73."

To which are added Three Letters, entitled "Miss Florence Cook's Mediumship," "Spirit-forms," and "The last of 'Katie King'"; the Photographing of 'Katie King' by the aid of the Electric Light.

James Burns, 15, Southampton Row, W.C.

8vo., 410 pp., Cloth, **3/6.**

HYPNOTISM.
BY
ALBERT MOLL (of Berlin).

Abridged Summary of Contents.

History of Hypnotism—General Considerations—Examples of Hypnosis—Terminology—Production of Hypnosis—Psychical Methods—Physical Methods—Combined Methods—Stages of Hypnosis—*Symptoms of Hypnosis*—Suggestion—Fascination—Catalepsy by Suggestion—Contractions—Ocular Symptoms—Objective Changes—Anatomical Changes—Estimation of Time, &c.—*Cognate States*—Somnambulism—Hypnosis in Animals—Fakirs, &c.—The Theory of Hypnotism—Simulation—The Medical Aspects of Hypnotism—The Legal Aspects of Hypnotism—Animal Magnetism—Index of Contents and Names—Bibliography.

8vo., 327 pp., Cloth, **3/6.**

PHYSIOGNOMY AND EXPRESSION.
By PAOLO MANTEGAZZA.

THE FEATURES OF THE HUMAN FACE:—The Forehead; Eyes; Eyebrows; Eyelashes; Nose; Mouth; Chin; Cheeks; Ears; Teeth; Hair and Beard; Moles; Wrinkles.

THE ALPHABET OF EXPRESSION:—Pleasure; Pain; Love and Benevolence; Devotion; Veneration; Hatred; Cruelty; Passion; Pride; Vanity; Fear; Thought; Racial and Professional Expression; Criteria for judging the moral and intellectual value of a Physiognomy, &c., &c.; Appendix; *Plates.*

James Burns, 15, Southampton Row, W.C.

INFORMATION FOR INVESTIGATORS.

Just Published, neat paper wrapper, post free, 2½d., or 1s. 9d. per doz.

MODERN SPIRITUALISM:
An Expository Sketch of its
Origin, Terminology, Phenomena, Method, Outcome
Dangers and Difficulties;
with Replies to Popular Objections.

By CHARLES WILLIAM DYMOND, F.S.A.

To which is appended Instructions to Investigators.

New Edition, Paper Wrapper, Price **2d**

THE PHILOSOPHY OF DEATH.
By ANDREW JACKSON DAVIS (CLAIRVOYANT).
Gives a Clairvoyant description of Death-bed Scenes, and the Condition of the Departed Spirit.

THEODORE PARKER IN SPIRIT-LIFE. A Narrative of Personal Experience given inspirationally to Dr. Willis. This little work gives a good view of life in the Spirit-World. New Edition. 1d.

LETTERS ON SPIRITUALISM. By Augustus Johnston, B.A., M.B., T.C.D. 4d.

RULES FOR THE SPIRIT-CIRCLE. By Emma Hardinge. 1d.

THE SPIRIT-CIRCLE AND THE LAWS OF MEDIUMSHIP. By Emma Hardinge. 1d.

SPIRITUALISM: Its Advantages to the Present and Future Life. By Mrs. C. L. V. Tappan. 1d.

MEDIUMS AND MEDIUMSHIP. By T. Hazard. 1d.

WHAT SPIRITUALISM HAS TAUGHT. William Howitt. 1d.

A SCIENTIFIC VIEW OF MODERN SPIRITUALISM. By T. Grant. 1d.

WHAT IS DEATH? By Hon. J. W. Edmonds. 1d.

NATURAL SPIRITUALISM. The Experiences of a Non-Spiritualist. 1d.

WHAT IS SPIRIT? An Essay on the Origin, Development, Attributes and Destiny of the Human Spirit. By C. Pine. 1d.

James Burns, 15, Southampton Row, W.C.

Price 8s. 6d.; Postage 6d.

PSYCHOMETRY.
A REVELATION OF THE
DIVINE POSSIBILITIES OF THE HUMAN SOUL,
AND INTELLECTUAL DAWN OF A NEW CIVILIZATION.

A Manual of the Philosophy, Science and Art, with Instructions for Students.

By JOSEPH RODES BUCHANAN, M.D.,

Professor of Physiology and Institutes of Medicine in four Medical Colleges successively, and Founder of Systematic Anthropology.

Embellished with a Portrait of Mrs. Buchanan.

Price 5s.; Postage 5d.

Life and Labour in the Spirit-World:
BEING A DESCRIPTION OF LOCALITIES, EMPLOYMENTS, SURROUNDINGS, AND CONDITIONS IN THE SPHERE.

By Members of the Spirit-band of Miss M. T. SHELHAMER.

WORKS OF EPES SARGENT.

Scientific Basis of Spiritualism. The author takes the ground, that since natural science is concerned with a knowledge of real phenomena, appealing to our sense-perceptions, and which are not only historically imparted, but are directly presented in the irresistible form of daily demonstrations to any faithful investigator, therefore Spiritualism is a natural science, and all opposition to it, under the ignorant pretence that it is outside of nature, is unscientific and unphilosophical. 6s. 6d.; *postage* 5d.

Proof Palpable of Immortality. Third edition—revised and corrected. Being an account of the Materialization Phenomena of Modern Spiritualism, with remarks on the relations of the Facts to Theology, Morals and Religion. Contains a wood-cut of the materialized spirit of "Katie King," from a photograph taken in London. 5s.; *p.* 3d.

Planchette; or, The Despair of Science. Being a full account of Modern Spiritualism, its phenomena and the various theories regarding it. With a survey of French Spiritism. 6s.; *postage* 3d.

WORKS OF KERSEY GRAVES.

Bible of Bibles; or, Twenty-Seven "Divine Revelations," containing a description of Twenty-Seven Bibles, and an Exposition of Two Thousand Biblical Errors in Science, History, Morals, Religion, and General Events. Also a Delineation of the Characters of the Principal Personages of the Christian Bible and an Examination of their Doctrines. 440 pp. 9s.; *postage* 5d.

World's Sixteen Crucified Saviors; or, Christianity Before Christ. Containing new and startling revelations in religious history, which disclose the Oriental origin of all the doctrines, principles, precepts and miracles of the Christian New Testament, and furnishing a key for unlocking many of its sacred mysteries, besides comprising the History of Sixteen Oriental Crucified Gods. 9s.; *p.* 5d.

Large 8vo., 1040 pp., Cloth, 21/-

Creative and Sexual Science;
Or, Manhood, Womanhood, and their Mutual Inter-relations; Love its Laws, Power, &c.; Selection, or Mutual Adaptation; Courtship; Married Life, &c., &c. By O. S. Fowler.

Large 8vo., 1211 pp., Illustrated, 21/-

Human Science;
Or, Phrenology, its Principles, Proofs, Faculties, Organs, Temperaments, Combinations, &c., applied to Health; its Value, Laws, Functions, &c., &c. By Prof. O. S. Fowler.

Plain Home Talk about the Human System; the Habits of Men and Women; the Cause and Prevention of Disease. Embracing Medical Common Sense applied to Society, Love, Marriage, Parentage, &c. By Edward B. Foote, M.D. 8vo., 959 pp., embellished with 200 illustrations, cloth, 6/-

Tokology. A Book for Every Woman. A new, popular, and interesting book upon Maternity. This pure book is written for the mothers and daughters of the land; written by a woman with a mother's inspiration, and warm with her love. By Alice B. Stockham, M.D. 8vo., illustrated, cloth, gilt, 8/-

The Science of a New Life. By John Cowan, M.D. Printed from beautifully clear, new type, on fine calendered, tinted paper, in 1 vol. of over 400 pages, 8vo., containing 100 first-class engravings. Bound in cloth, bevelled boards, gilt, 12/-

Parturition Without Pain; or, a Code of Directions for avoiding most of the Pains and Dangers of Child-Bearing. Cloth, 4/-

How to Feed the Baby, to make it Healthy and Happy; with Health Hints. By C. E. Page, M.D. Sixth Edition. Paper, 2/-

The True Healing Art: or, Hygienic *versus* Drug Medication. By R. T. Trall, M.D. 1/-

The Relations of the Sexes. By Mrs. E. B. Duffey. Cloth, 5/-

Love, Courtship and Marriage. By R. B. D. Wells. Paper, 1/6.

Woman: Her Diseases, and how to Cure them. By R. B. D. Wells. Paper, 1/6.

James Burns, 15, Southampton Row, W.C.

Your Luck's in Your Hand; or, the Science of Modern Palmistry, chiefly according to the System of D'Arpentigny and Desbarrolles, with some account of the Gipsies. By A. R. CRAIG, M.A. Third Edition, with five illustrations. 3s. 6d.

The Psychonomy of the Hand; or, the Hand an Index of Mental Development, according to MM. D'Arpentigny and Desbarrolles, with illustrative tracings from living hands. By RICHARD BEAMISH, F.R.S., &c. Second Edition. 7s. 6d.

The Handbook of Palmistry and Physiognomy. Illustrated. By ROSA BAUGHAN. 3s. 6d.

The Handbook of Physiognomy. By Rosa Baughan. 1s.

Chiromancy; or, The Science of Palmistry. Being a Concise Exposition of the Principles and Practice of the Art of Reading the Hand, by which the Past, the Present, and the Future may be explained and foretold. Illustrated. Cloth, 1s.

Mother Shipton Investigated. The result of critical examination, in the British Museum Library, of the literature relating to the Yorkshire Sybil. By WM. H. HARRISON. 1s.

Spiritualism; Its Facts and Phases. Illustrated with Personal Experiences and Fac-similes of Spirit-Writing. By J. H. Powell. 2s.

Theosophy, Religion and Occult Science. By HENRY S. OLCOTT. 7s 6d.

Another World; or, Fragments from the Star City of Montalluyah. By HERMES. Second edition. 3s.

The Story of a Great Delusion in a series of matter-of-fact chapters. [Anti-Vaccination.] By WILLIAM WHITE. 4s. 6d.

Light on the Path: A Treatise written for the personal use of those who are ignorant of the Eastern Wisdom, and who desire to enter within its influence, written down by M. C. Square 12 mo., cloth, 1s. 6d.

Raphael's Horary Astrology; by which every question relating to the future may be answered. By RAPHAEL. In 3 Vols. 3s. each.

Other-World Order: Suggestions and Conclusions thereon. By Wm. White. 3s.

The Church of Christ not an Ecclesiasticism. By Henry James. Second Edition. 1s.

The Origin and Destiny of Britain. By H. Brittain, F.SA 1s.

Physiology for Schools. In twenty-seven easy Lessons. By Mrs. Charles Bray. Third Edition. 1s.

Woman and a Future Life. 2s. 6d.

Notes of an Enquiry into the Phenomena called Spiritual. By WM. CROOKES, F.R.S., &c. 1s.

On the Connection of Christianity with Solar Worship. Translated from DUPUIS, by T. E. PARTRIDGE. 1s.

The Philosophy of Man: A golden handbook for all. By P. DAVIDSON. 1s.

Handsome Cloth, **4/-** *Illustrated Paper Wrappers,* **2/6.**
(*Post Free in both cases.*)

HUMAN FACES: WHAT THEY MEAN!
Or, How to Read Character.
By JOSEPH SIMMS, M.D.
Author of "Physiognomy Illustrated; or, Nature's Revelations of Character."

1. Charlemagne; 2. Boswell; 3. Cingalese; 4. Locke; 5. Tasmanian; 6. Byron;
7. Caius Cassius; 8. Rev. Rowland Hill; 9. Lavater; 10. Paul I., Emperor of Russia.

768 pp., over 1000 *Illustrations,* **£1.**

NEW PHYSIOGNOMY:
Or, Signs of Character, as Manifested through Temperament and External Forms, and especially in the "Human Face Divine."
By SAMUEL R. WELLS.

200 pp., 200 *Illustrations,* **2/-** *Extra edition, Cloth,* **4/-**
Heads and Faces: How to Study Them.
By NELSON SIZER and H. S. DRAYTON, M.D.

8vo., 168 *pp., Cloth,* **4/-**
HUMAN MAGNETISM;
Its Nature, Physiology and Psychology. By H. S. Drayton.

The aim of the author in preparing this volume is to furnish the general reader with a summary of principles and facts bearing upon the subject of magnetism, and to furnish them in a manner as free as possible from prejudice or partiality.

James Burns, 15, Southampton Row, W.C.

ANOTHER WORLD:
Or, Fragments from the Star City of Montalluyah. By Hermes.
Second Edition, 5/-

SIRENIA:
Or, Recollections of a Past Existence. Second Edition. 2/6.

Hafed. Prince of Persia; his Experiences in Earth-Life and Spirit-Life; being Communications received through Mr. David Duguid, the Glasgow trance-painting Medium. *Illustrated* 6/-
Hermes, a Disciple of Jesus: his Life and Missionary Work; also the Evangelistic Travels of Anah and Zitha. A Sequel to "Hafed" 6/6
Outside the Gates: and other Tales and Sketches. By a Band of Spirit-Intelligences, through the Mediumship of Miss M. T. Shelhamer 5/6
Epitome of Spiritualism and Spirit-Magnetism. Their Verity, Practicability, Conditions and Laws. Paper 1/6
Heaven Revised; a Narrative of Personal Experiences after the change called Death. By Mrs. E. B. Duffey. Paper 1/-
Defence of Modern Spiritualism. By A. R. Wallace, F.R.S., with American Preface by Epes Sargent. Paper .. 1/-
Character Indicated by Handwriting. A Practical Treatise in support of the assertion that the Handwriting of a person is an infallible guide to his character. By Rosa Baughan. 2nd edition 3/6
Human Immortality Proved by Facts. Report of a Two Nights' Debate on Modern Spiritualism, between C. Bradlaugh and J. Burns. Paper .. .. 6d.
Physiognomy Illustrated, or Nature's Revelations of Character. By Joseph Simms, M.D. Complete in 1 Vol. *Fully Illustrated* 10/6

MR. BURNS will furnish his SPECIAL CATALOGUES of Works on Spiritualism, Mesmerism, Hypnotism, Palmistry, Theosophy, Occultism, Phrenology, Physiology, Hygiene, &c. free on application.

☞ A Catalogue of Second-hand Works on the above Subjects is published periodically, and is supplied post free for one stamp.

MR. BURNS has the most Varied and Extensive Stock, in these particular branches, of any European dealer.

James Burns, 15, Southampton Row, W.C.

www.ingramcontent.com/pod-product-compliance
Lightning Source LLC
Chambersburg PA
CBHW031336230426
43670CB00006B/350